## Praise for Ken Dwight and

I'm as average and unlearned a compute... ...
has come to depend on the thing, and needs to trust it while still
maximizing its potential. Thank you, Ken, for this clear and
concise how-to on caring for my machine, keeping it safe and my
work intact.

*— Rev. Dr. Jesse Jennings*

Ken has attacked this important subject and created a "Must
Have" book for every computer owner. It is a timely, informative
and extremely readable book on computer protection. This book
may just save you from the perils of personal data loss and potential identity theft.

*— Dale Liu, Sr. Security Consultant/Trainer*
*Computer Revolution Enterprises*

Most people find that they have to use computers to get through
the day these days. For the first time in history they are using a
technology they hardly understand and increasingly fear. Not
understanding the technology because of its gobbledygook
language, and fearing it because, like some medieval plague it has
virus epidemics causing global horror diseases such as personal
eavesdropping and loss of identity.

At last we have a book that translates the gobbledygook and takes
away the fear in one masterful stroke.

Ken Dwight is a veritable Louis Pasteur, he gives us the cure for a
scourge simply by making the computer virus a beatable
disease.

His Book *Bug-Free Computing* should be on every computer
operator's desk - worldwide. Just like me - I want my computer to
live a healthy lifestyle.

*Michael Hick*
*Author "GLOBAL DEALS - Marketing and Managing Across*
*Cultural Frontiers"*

The cause and the cure for viruses and other malware can be
found in here. Most books leave me with more questions. This
book has the answers!

*Louis Lopez, MSCE, CNE, CCNA, CCA, MCP+I, A+, N+, CCSA,*
*CCSE, ICIS, Intel StorageWorks Specialist, HP STAR ISP, NCP,*
*NTP, Compaq ASE*

Ken Dwight's writing is brilliant in its intelligence and analysis, yet a very comfortable read for layman computer operators, like me. For the computer users who use the Internet minutes a day in fun and communication, to the professionals in all disciplines who are now so dependent upon computers for their productivity and livelihood, this book is invaluable.

*Douglas Shannon,*
*General Manager, Northgate Forest Companies*

If you think you know it all about protecting your computer from viruses, spyware and hackers, think again. This book will help take the fear out of potential dangers lurking on the Internet and help shield you from malicious attacks. The Virus Doctor knows what is best and explains it in an easy-to-read book.

*Michael Garfield, "The High-Tech Texan®"*
*Technology Radio and TV Host*

If you rely on your computer to help run your business, this book is a must-read. It offers valuable advice on how to protect your data. Best of all the information has been "translated" from GEEK into easy-to-understand language. It's easy to see how an ounce of prevention can save your computer data...and your business.

*Tom Britton, President*
*Greater Heights Chamber of Commerce*

This book perfectly serves the needs of two markets – it's required reading for my technicians, who are frequently required to identify and remove viruses, spyware, and other malicious programs from client computers, and we recommend the book to all of our clients, to help them prevent these problems from infecting their computers in the future.

*Wayne Springer, President*
*Atiwa Computing, Inc.*

It is with great pleasure that I endorse your new book, *Bug-Free Computing*. It is excellent and timely. I totally agree with your statement that "there are only two kinds of computers in use today – those that have been infected by a virus, and those that will be!" In my 2005 edition of *Stress Management: A Comprehensive Guide to Wellness* (Ballantine, New York) I dedicated a new chapter to "Technology and Time Management: Focus Your Laser." One of my statements is: "Unfortunately, there are many "big, bad wolves" out there that can make our high technology time management techniques more stress promoting than stress managing. We can make a mistake, technology can fail, electricity can surge and viruses can sabotage." You can bet that my next edition will reference *Bug-Free Computing* to help my readers have another resource to help them cope with the stress of our high technology era. Best of luck in your publishing venture and thanks for helping others protect themselves from the "big, bad wolves" and manage their stress more effectively.

*Edward A. Charlesworth, PhD*
*Clinical Psychologist*
*Co-Author of "Stress Management: A Comprehensive Guide to*
*Wellness" (Ballantine, New York)*

# Bug-Free Computing

## Stop Viruses, Squash Worms, and Smash Trojan Horses

## Ken Dwight

Copyright ©2005

The TeleProcessors, Inc.

Houston, Texas U.S.A.

Bug-Free Computing™
Stop Viruses, Squash Worms, and Smash Trojan Horses

By Ken Dwight, "The Virus Docror™"

Published by:
The TeleProcessors, Inc.
14300 Cornerstone Village Drive, Suite 321
Houston, TX 77014-1276

info@thevirusdoc.com
www.thevirusdoc.com

Copyright © 2005 by Ken Dwight

First Printing: October, 2005

ISBN, print ed.        0-9754085-4-2

The paper used in this publication meets the requirements of the American National Standard for Permanence of Paper for Printed Library Materials Z39.48-1984.

Printed in the United States of America

# Contents

Acknowledgments and Dedication ................................................................i

About the Author .......................................................................................iii

Prologue ..................................................................................................... v

How To Use This Book .............................................................................. vii

Chapter 1: Why You Need To Read This Book ............................................1

Chapter 2: Facts About the Current Generation of Viruses .......................5

Chapter 3: What the Anti-Virus Software Vendors Won't Tell You ........... 11

Chapter 4: Definitions, Common Viruses, Evolution of the Threat .......... 13

Chapter 5: Who Writes Viruses, and Why? .................................................23

Chapter 6: The Importance of Backups .....................................................33

Chapter 7: Kinds of Damage Viruses May Cause ......................................47

Chapter 8: How Viruses Are Spread ..........................................................53

Chapter 9: Dealing With Spam ..................................................................61

Chapter 10: Other Forms of Malware ........................................................87

Chapter 11: Anti-Virus and Firewall Software .......................................... 107

Chapter 12: Reading E-Mail Headers ....................................................... 113

Chapter 13: Preventive Measures .............................................................. 119

Chapter 14: Recognizing Virus Behavior .................................................. 131

Chapter 15: What to Do if Your Computer Is Infected ............................ 157

Appendix A: Country Codes, Listed Alphabetically ................................. 163

Appendix B: Unsafe File List, from Microsoft ......................................... 167

Appendix C: Keeping This Information Current....................................... 169

# Acknowledgments and Dedication

As a first-time author, I had no idea how many pieces had to come together to produce a book suitable for widespread public consumption. From the first outline of the manuscript to the finished product you see here today, dozens of hands, minds, and checkbooks have contributed to this effort.

It would be impossible to rank these individuals in terms of their participation, so I will simply list them in alphabetical order. Some helped with the technical aspects of the book, some with moral support and inspiration, and some invested their hard-earned dollars in bringing this project to fruition. And obviously, many of these special people contributed in all of these areas. Here are those names:

Marcene Adams
Ron Boehm
Grace and Wayne
    Carpenter
Gail Coco
Dr. Mack Elbert Coker
Bill Cowles
Don Crawley
Vicky and Ernest Dwight
Mary Jo and Ron Eggers
Marian Eide
Barbara Fielder
Michael Garfield
Cindy Guire
Ed Holtgraver
Larry Hoole

Rev. Dr. Jesse Jennings
Marcia and Ed Jones
Jon Joseph
Dr. Diane Kane
Sabah Kobersi
Linda Larsen
Dale Liu
Marilyn Manning
Mac McKinney
Rita Mills
Mary and Scott Moore
Michelle Nichols
Susan O'Neal
Chris O'Shea
Stefani and Mike Palmer
Dan Poynter

Kathy Roberson
Louella and Wayne Roush
Meryl Runion
Steve Schmid
Cindy and Doug Shannon
Patsi and Michael Sheets
Dwight Silverman
Wayne Springer
Charlie Thorp
Bob Tuttle
Barney Zick

Finally, I dedicate this book to the memory of my loving parents, Mary C. Dwight (1916-2005) and Kennedy B. Dwight (1916-2000), without whom none of this would have been possible.

# About the Author

**Ken Dwight** has been a computer professional since 1966, when he was hired as a Programmer Trainee on mainframe computers. Riding the IT fast track, he held numerous positions over the next six years, including Systems Analyst, Systems Programmer, and Senior Systems Engineer for a leading computer terminal manufacturer.

In 1972 he left the corporate world to start his consulting practice, The TeleProcessors, Inc., which he still serves today as President. In 1982, his firm bought its first IBM Personal Computer, and the focus of the consulting practice since then has been primarily PC related.

Ken spends more than 100 days per year teaching Advanced PC Troubleshooting in two-day seminars around the United States, as well as the United Kingdom and Australia.

Since 2002, when the Klez worm changed the landscape of computer viruses, Ken has specialized in preventing, curing, and repairing the damage caused by malware on Personal Computers. Known as The Virus Doctor™, Ken is recognized today as one of the leading authorities on this ever-changing subject.

In order to educate the computer-using public, he developed the seminar, *All About Computer Viruses,* and the in-depth *Computer Virus Boot Camp.* These seminars are held in major cities around the United States and will be coming soon to Canada, the United Kingdom, Australia, and New Zealand.

With this, his first book, Ken is offering this vital information to those computer users who can't attend a live seminar, or those attendees who want even more detailed information on this rapidly changing subject.

# Prologue

There are still some otherwise knowledgeable, experienced computer users who don't understand the need for a book like this. They haven't had the experience of seeing their computer become infected by a virus, or dealt with the repercussions of this potentially catastrophic event.

Unfortunately, it can be safely said that there are only two kinds of computers in use today – those that have been infected by a virus, and those that will be! In today's computing environment, every computer is exposed to viruses and other potentially destructive malware on a regular basis. It's only a matter of time until any computer becomes infected.

One purpose of this book is to remove the complacency that affects most computer users, especially those who haven't yet had this life-changing experience. In the process, we will explode some of the myths on the subject, and open the reader's eyes to the myriad of ways these destructive pieces of software can travel from one computer to another, and the various forms of damage they may cause.

The intended audience for this book is the typical computer user, although it provides essential background information for computer technicians as well. The book is deliberately written in plain English, with as little in the way of jargon, buzzwords, and TLAs as possible.

If you're not familiar with TLAs, those are a standard part of the computer person's vocabulary. The letters represent Three-Letter Acronyms, which can be found throughout any computer manual. Think FDC, HDD, ISA, MHz, PCI, RAM, ROM, USB, and on and on. You won't find many of those in this book!

# How To Use This Book

This book is organized in such a way as to be read from start to finish. Each chapter builds upon the information presented up to that point, to give the reader a thorough understanding of the subject.

But depending on your particular circumstances, you may want to start at some point other than the beginning, to solve a problem or resolve an issue that you consider the most urgent. Here are a few possible scenarios.

If you suspect that your computer may already be infected by a virus, or if you know for a fact that it is, you may want to go right to Chapter 14, "Recognizing Virus Behavior," and confirm or refute your suspicion. If you determine that the computer is infected, proceed directly to Chapter 15, "What to Do if Your Computer Is Infected."

If you decide that your top priority is to protect your computer from virus infection right away, you may want to start with Chapter 13, "Preventive Measures," and follow the procedures listed there. Then you can go back and learn about viruses at a more leisurely pace, knowing that your system is protected from most of these threats.

You may already understand the importance of backing up your computer and its critical data files, but know you're not taking the most effective approach to this vital operation. To give yourself that peace of mind, you may want to study Chapter 6, "The Importance of Backups," and establish backup procedures that will allow you to recover from a worst-case scenario.

If your main concern is slowing the flow of spam that fills your Inbox every morning, Chapter 9, "Dealing With Spam," will be your top priority. This chapter shows you how to use the message filtering provided by your Internet Service Provider and your e-mail program as your first line of defense against these annoying productivity killers. For a more aggressive approach to reducing spam input, this chapter discusses add-on programs that give you many more options.

Finally, if you're one of those brave (some would say foolhardy) individuals who doesn't have anti-virus software installed on your computer, you certainly want to go directly to Chapter 11, "Anti-Virus and Firewall Software," and explore your alternatives for providing this critical element of protection. If you've been reluctant to spend the money for a shrink-wrapped, commercial anti-virus software package, this chapter lists several such programs that are available to you at no cost. Choosing one of these products instead of the more popular ones you'll find on the shelves of your local computer store can easily save you more money than you spent to buy this book!

# Chapter 1
## Why You Need To Read This Book

If you've never experienced the sinking feeling that comes from knowing your computer has been infected by a virus, you may be somewhat puzzled by all the hysteria that follows whenever a new virus outbreak is announced. If you're in this ever-diminishing category of computer users, you may not consider a virus to be a significant threat.

Typical computer users frequently have this attitude for several reasons. See how many of these describe your feelings on the subject:

- I'm not at risk of contracting a virus, because my computer came with an anti-virus program already installed.
- I'm not at risk of contracting a virus, because I don't open attachments from people I don't know.
- If my computer does become virus infected, I'll just call my computer technician to get rid of it.

The sense of security expressed in these statements is no longer justified in today's virus environment, though. Here are the fallacies of those statements:

- Simply having an AV program installed on your computer is not sufficient protection against most modern viruses; most computers that fall prey to virus infection actually had AV software installed at the time they became infected.
- Viruses now spread in many ways that do not require attachments, or even e-mail messages at all; and when a virus does spread via e-mail, the virus-infected message will usually appear to come from someone you know.
- While a qualified computer technician can repair most of the damage caused by a virus infection, there are some forms of virus-inflicted damage that cannot be undone. As in so many other areas of life, prevention is far more effective and less expensive than a cure.

As these simple examples illustrate, the virus problem has become much more complicated over the past few years, to the point that the "conventional wisdom" on virus prevention is of little value these days. And removing a virus that has infected your computer may be extremely difficult, if not impossible, even for the most knowledgeable and experienced computer technician.

It's safe to say that almost everything about viruses has changed in the past few years. To illustrate that point, here are some of the changes that affect your exposure to the current generation of viruses:

- Who produces them
- Why they do it
- How they infect a computer
- How they spread from one computer to another
- Types of damage they cause
- Symptoms of virus infection
- How to prevent them from infecting your computer
- How to remove them from an infected computer

The remaining chapters of this book will provide a more detailed look at these changes and how they affect your exposure to viruses, worms, and other forms of malware. As you can see, the virus landscape in 2005 is much different from what it was in 2002.

If you haven't given it much thought before now, consider what could be at stake if a virus infects your computer. The consequences fall into several major categories:

- You may lose files that will need to be recreated, through manual data entry.
- You may not be able to recreate some historical information, which could be lost forever.
- There will certainly be a dollar cost to repair virus damage, restore deleted or damaged programs and data files, and reduce the likelihood of future losses.
- Your business could lose revenue if it cannot function until the damage is repaired.

This final category needs to receive special emphasis, because this single factor could be devastating to your business. A detailed study by the highly regarded Gartner Group found that, of businesses that lose their computer systems for five business days, 70 percent never recover; that figure climbs to over 90 percent if the loss of computers exceeds ten business days. In other words, a serious virus infestation could, quite literally, cost you your business!

Consider some of the specific damages you could incur as a result of a virus:

- Deleted files and/or programs
- Confidential information freely distributed
- Theft of credit card numbers, passwords, customer lists, business plans, etc.
- Liability exposure if others are infected by a virus from your computer
- Damage to your company's reputation and credibility

As you can see, the threat posed by viruses is much more than a nuisance or an inconvenience. Your whole business is at stake.

# Chapter 2
## Facts About the Current Generation of Viruses

Since the whole virus landscape has changed so dramatically over the past few years, it's worth taking a few minutes to bring you up to date on the current state of the virus writers' art. Some of these facts may shock you; that is the intent of this chapter.

## Likelihood of Infection

Perhaps the most important fact to bear in mind is that virus infections are at an all-time high. Although the exact numbers vary widely from month to month, in any given month millions of computers become infected. This is not a reference to the number of computers that are exposed to viruses; that number is many times higher. This statistic represents only the computers that actually become infected by a virus.

If you use your computer to send and receive e-mail, or if it's connected to the Internet, it's a virtual certainty that you will be sent at least one virus every week; many users are dealing with dozens, even hundreds, of viruses trying to infect their computer every day. There are a number of factors that determine your level of exposure, which will be covered in detail in Chapter 13, "Preventive Measures."

As you may have realized by now, having a virus infect your computer can be every bit as catastrophic to your business as having the computer stolen, or destroyed in a natural disaster such as a fire or a flood. You can't afford to ignore the threat.

## Cost of Infection

Speaking of what you can and can't afford, it would be helpful to examine the cost of virus damage to computer systems, worldwide. Unfortunately, there are no reliable statistics to identify the total dollar cost, for several reasons.

One problem is that most likely sources of such statistics have a vested interest in making those numbers as high as possible. One article, published in 2000, estimated the total worldwide cost of virus infection that year at $1.5 trillion. Clearly, that number would not stand up to any serious scrutiny, as it is equivalent to the gross national product of most industrialized nations!

But most major corporations can closely estimate the cost of computer downtime, in terms of dollars of lost productivity per minute. At a given company, even a single hour without access to its computer network, when multiplied by hundreds or thousands of employees on the clock, easily runs into the thousands or tens of thousands of dollars.

Now measure that downtime in days instead of hours, and multiply this one organization by the thousands of businesses that are infected by viruses every month. Just the cost of lost productivity easily runs into billions of dollars per month.

Another way to measure the cost of virus infections would be to calculate the number of technician hours required to repair the damage caused by a particular virus, and to restore, repair, or recreate the damaged program and data files. Taking those hours and multiplying them by a prevailing, fully burdened wage produces a hard dollar figure that can be used in this discussion.

Even an approach such as this, however, overlooks a critical factor in the equation. That is the fact that large organizations are already paying the technicians to be there, so this is not actually a direct labor cost. The virus repair may take staff time away from their other responsibilities, but it does not represent an incremental cost.

What can be clearly measured, though, is the direct cost to small businesses and individuals who, not having an IT staff or technical support personnel on the payroll, must pay those people an on-demand hourly rate to resolve these problems. Those numbers are much easier to calculate.

Even a simple virus infection can be expected to require a minimum of two hours' work by a trained technician to identify and repair the damage, and to protect the computer from becoming reinfected. That figure can easily rise to five or ten, or even more hours on a single computer, depending on the nature and severity of the infection.

If we assume an unrealistically low hourly rate for a technician with the skills required to competently perform this work, six or seven hours of this person's time would approximate the cost of a new computer; assuming a more realistic rate, that break-even point comes at about the four-hour mark.

In other words, there are many times when the most cost-effective way to deal with a virus-infected computer is to replace it with a new one, and not even try to repair the damage done to the old system. Of course, even in that scenario, it will probably still be necessary to retrieve the data files from the old computer and rid them of any viruses before installing those files on the new system.

## Infection Methods

With these depressing statistics as the background, this chapter will conclude with some of the nastiest surprises about the current environment of viruses. Most of these are important changes that have taken place over the past few years.

Probably the most frequent surprise faced by many computer users is the fact that their computer has become infected, even though it had anti-virus software installed. As you'll discover in Chapter 13, "Preventive Measures," it takes much more than an anti-virus program to keep your computer from becoming infected. In fact, a high percentage of infected computers do have an anti-virus program installed at the time of the infection.

Another distressing difference in many of the modern viruses is that they may exhibit no obvious symptoms when they first infect your computer. Many of these devious programs run in the background, silently doing their damage, without letting you know there is a problem. By the time the damage becomes obvious, it may be too extensive to be economically repairable. That's one more reason that prevention has become so important.

As with so many aspects of the computer industry, the "conventional wisdom" can hurt you if you don't stay up to date. A perfect example of this problem is the assumption that your computer is not susceptible to virus infection unless you open an attachment to an e-mail message.

Where older viruses required that the computer user open an attachment in order for their computer to become infected, that step is no longer necessary. Several years ago, the virus writers developed a technique that causes the virus to infect a system as soon as the e-mail message containing the virus is opened. We discuss this issue in greater detail in Chapter 8, "How Viruses Are Spread."

Another example of old information that no longer protects you is the source of an e-mail message that could contain a virus. While you were safe a few years ago if you didn't open an e-mail from someone you didn't know, you can no longer trust the sender's name or the e-mail address you see in the "From" field of an e-mail message.

Most virus writers today "spoof" that address, so that the infected message may appear to come from someone you know and trust. Especially if there's an attachment involved, it's prudent to be suspicious of any e-mail you weren't expecting, even if it apparently comes from someone you know.

## Distribution Methods

The way that viruses spread from one infected computer to another has also changed dramatically in recent years. While early viruses examined the Address Book of the infected computer to find additional e-mail addresses to target for infection, modern viruses have become far more sophisticated.

The current crop of viruses will search for e-mail addresses in multiple locations on the infected computer, including saved e-mail messages, Microsoft Excel spreadsheets, Microsoft Word documents, Microsoft Access databases, and other likely places that e-mail addresses may reside. This technique is described in greater detail in Chapter 8, "How Viruses Are Spread."

One of the more recent developments in the virus-writers' trade was demonstrated, very convincingly, by the Blaster worm. Unlike virtually all viruses in the past, Blaster did not come into target computers through an e-mail message. Or through a chat room, or an Instant Messaging system. Or by clicking on a link in a Web page.

Instead, Blaster selected its targets by randomly generating computer addresses (technically, IP Addresses) and sending itself to those addresses. If your computer happened to be connected to the Internet at an address that matched one of those generated by the instructions in Blaster, you received the worm without asking for it in any way. Within days of its introduction, the Blaster worm had infected hundreds of thousands of computers, worldwide.

Those are some of the little-known facts about viruses in today's computing world. Table 2.1 provides a brief summary of these facts and statistics. Did you know about all of those changes? See why it's important to read the rest of this book? Good!

## Table 2.1 Computer Virus Facts:

1. The rate of virus infection is at an all-time high; millions of computers become infected every month.

2. Virtually every e-mail user will receive a virus this month (and every month)!

3. Having a virus infect your computer can be every bit as catastrophic as if the computer were stolen or destroyed in a fire or flood.

4. The annual cost of recovering from virus damage is certainly in the billions of dollars; the Sasser outbreak in 2004 was estimated to have caused $15 billion in damage in less than 30 days.

5. The cost of repairing virus damage can easily exceed the cost of buying a new computer; minimum cost of a simple virus repair is usually two hours of labor.

6. Most infected computers had antivirus software installed at the time of the infection.

7. Modern viruses may exhibit no obvious symptoms of infection for days, weeks, or even months after infection; they just do their damage in the background, while the host suspects nothing.

8. It is not necessary to open an attachment in order to become infected by a virus.

9. Virus-infected e-mail messages will frequently appear to come from someone you know.

10. Some viruses don't come through e-mail, Web sites, or other "traditional" means of infection. The first prominent example was the Blaster worm; more recently, Sasser used this distribution method.

# Chapter 3
## What the Anti-Virus Software
## Vendors Won't Tell You

The companies that are in the business of selling anti-virus software (we'll shorten that to AV software for the remainder of this book) would like for you to think that buying and installing their product is all you need to do to protect your computer from virus infection. Unfortunately, that perception is not accurate.

A large percentage of the computers that become infected by a virus did, in fact, have an AV program installed at the time of infection. That fact should serve as sufficient evidence of the need for more than AV software to block the threat.

In Chapter 13, "Preventive Measures," we will cover step-by-step the procedures you need to follow in order to reduce the virus threat as much as is reasonably possible. But this is a good time to point out some of the inherent limitations of AV programs.

First, you need to always be aware of the changing nature of the virus landscape. Every week, new viruses are introduced and start spreading around the world. In addition to new viruses, the virus writers will sometimes devise a new method of causing damage to the data stored on your computer system.

If your AV program doesn't know about these new viruses, or the new techniques they might use to cause you harm, the program can't protect your computer from these threats. It's critically important to keep the virus definitions up to date on your AV program. Most of these products make it easy to keep them updated; in many cases, they can be set up to automatically download the updates on a regular basis.

Another possible loophole that can defeat any AV program is not having the scanning options set properly. Your options should be set to scan every incoming e-mail message and every attachment before that data is allowed onto your hard drive. Most AV programs set up automatic scanning by default, but you need to be sure your software has those options enabled.

Another concern arises when the incoming virus is carrying a Worm, or a Trojan horse. These terms are defined in Chapter 4, "Definitions, Common Viruses, Evolution of the Threat," but the point here is that your AV program may not automatically detect some of these malevolent programs. Detection of Worms and Trojan horses has been improved in later versions of AV software. This improvement is a good reason to consider updating your AV software.

# Chapter 4
## Definitions, Common Viruses, Evolution of the Threat

Computer viruses have been around since the 1980s, although they have become a serious threat to most computer users only since the late 1990s. When the term "Computer Virus" is used in most conversations, it actually encompasses several different kinds of threats that might infect your computer.

Here are working definitions of some of the terms that will be used in this book, and the effect they may have on your computer systems. Some of these definitions are based on those found on the Symantec and Microsoft Web sites:

Malware – Any program that was written specifically for the purpose of damaging a computer system. These programs were designed and distributed with malevolent intent, and serve no useful purpose for the computer user. This is a generic term that includes the specific types of programs that follow.

Virus – A program or code that replicates, that is, infects another program, boot sector, partition, or document that supports macros by inserting itself or attaching itself to that medium. Most viruses just replicate; many also cause damage.

Worm – A subclass of virus. A program that makes copies of itself, for example from one disk drive to another. It may do damage and compromise the security of the computer. A worm can consume memory or network bandwidth, thus causing a computer to stop responding. It may arrive in the form of a joke program, a screen saver, or some other type of software.

Trojan Horse – A program that neither replicates or copies itself, but does damage or compromises the security of the computer. Typically it relies on someone e-mailing it to you, it does not email itself. Also may be downloaded without your knowledge or consent, along with other software that appears to be desirable.

**Spam** – Unsolicited commercial e-mail advertising, also known as UCE. Certainly the most annoying type of incoming e-mail message, although spam doesn't technically meet the definition of malware. Occasionally, you may receive something useful from a spam message.

**Spyware** – A program that is loaded on your computer, usually without your knowledge, for the purpose of monitoring your activities on the Internet and reporting those activities to the entity responsible for placing the spyware on your computer. The most common use of spyware is to send you more spam, promoting products or services that appear to hold some interest to you.

In reviewing the descriptions of specific viruses, you may find reference to certain types of virus. These are two categories of virus that present their own, unique set of problems:

**Macro virus** – A program or code segment written in the internal macro language of an application, such as Microsoft Word or Excel. Some macros replicate, while others simply infect documents, worksheets, or templates.

**Polymorphic virus** – A virus that has the ability to change its byte pattern when it replicates, thereby avoiding detection by simple string-scanning techniques.

It is also common to find certain abbreviations or acronyms in the name of a given virus. These are the most common in modern viruses:

**W32** – Designates the type of virus according to the target platform as 32-bit Windows, or Linux or Mac.

**@mm** – Signifies the virus or worm is a "mass-mailer." An example is Melissa, which sends messages to every e-mail address in your mailbox. A more recent example is Sobig.F, which sends messages to every e-mail address it finds on an infected computer, especially those addresses contained in other e-mail messages.

**HLLW** – Signifies this piece of malware is a High-Level Language Worm, meaning that the Worm is written in a programming language with advanced capabilities.

The remaining definitions come from the Symantec Web site, and describe the characteristics of a specific virus threat. Since most AV software vendors use similar terms in their documentation and on their Web sites, these may serve as a representative listing:

**Distribution** – This component measures how quickly a threat is able to spread itself.

**Payload** – This is the malicious activity that the virus performs. Not all viruses have payloads, but there are some that perform destructive actions.

**Payload Trigger** – This is the condition that causes the virus to activate or drop its destructive payload. Some viruses trigger their payloads on a certain date. Others might trigger their payload based on the execution of certain programs or the availability of an Internet connection.

Finally, these terms define the severity of the threat posed by this specific piece of malware. At a glance, they give you a concise indication of the degree of damage your computer may have suffered, the difficulty of repairing the damage caused by this threat, and the likelihood of preventing further infection and distribution:

**Threat Assessment** – This is a severity rating of the virus, worm, or Trojan horse. It includes the damage that this threat causes, how quickly it can spread to other computers (distribution), and how widespread the infections are known to be (wild).

**Threat Containment** – This is a measure of how well current antivirus technology can keep this threat from spreading. As a general rule, older virus techniques are generally well contained; new threat types or highly complex viruses can be more difficult to contain, and are correspondingly more a threat to the user community. The measures are Easy (the threat is well-contained), Moderate (the threat is partially contained), and Difficult (the threat is not currently containable).

**Wild** – The wild component measures the extent to which a virus is already spreading among computer users. This measurement includes the number of independent sites infected, the number of computers infected, the geographic distribution of infection, the ability of current technology to combat the threat, and the complexity of the virus.

---

# A Brief History of Computer Viruses
## The First Generation

The first computer virus was introduced in 1988, and the threat posed by viruses has been a serious concern for average computer users since the late 1990s. While the risk of your computer becoming infected by a virus was fairly low until a few years ago, the likelihood of your computer being exposed to a virus today is virtually assured.

In the early days of computer viruses, these programs were spread by means of floppy disks being passed from one infected machine to another. There was no Internet to be used as a distribution medium, and even Local Area Networks, or LANs, were uncommon in small businesses and undreamed of in the home.

## Later in The First Generation

The second method of virus distribution was a statistically unlikely event, which was by way of an infected CD-ROM disk. At the time, CD recorders were too expensive for most computer users to have access to them, so it was a rare virus writer who could spread the damage via this medium. There were actually a few cases of infected CD-ROM disks coming from software vendors, but those disks were quickly identified and replaced.

## The Second Generation

Prior to the popularity of LANs, most examples of virus infestation that made the newspapers or the nightly television news were in large organizations. Those were the only places with networks installed, where the virus could spread rapidly and across multiple locations. Once the virus writers developed the programming techniques to propagate across networks, the dramatic rise in rates of virus infection began.

Today, most businesses of any size, as well as many homes, have multiple computers connected through a LAN. If a virus infects one computer on your LAN, you can count on that virus spreading to the other computers in short order, unless you have taken proactive steps to protect them.

## The Third Generation – Viruses in Today's Environment

Of course, the Internet and e-mail are the answer to any virus writer's prayers. In today's connected world, any new virus can spread to millions of computers in mere minutes from the time of its introduction to the Internet. That's why it's so important for you to have preventive measures in place, to protect your computer systems from the multitude of ways they may be targeted today.

It's becoming harder to stay ahead of the virus writers in protecting our systems against new viruses as they evolve. One reason for this difficulty is the fact that virus writers communicate with one another, and build upon successful techniques. This culture has its own Web sites, chat rooms, "how-to" manuals, and even conventions and other face-to-face meetings. When a virus introduces a new method of distributing itself more efficiently or effectively, or causing new forms of damage to an infected system, you need to assume that these approaches will become the new standard. In other words, the virus writers are continually "raising the bar" of the destruction they cause.

Here are some examples of techniques that were groundbreaking when first introduced, which can now be expected in any new viruses. Some of these have been mentioned earlier, but this context will more clearly illustrate the evolution of virus behavior.

When viruses first incorporated the ability to spread from one drive to another, that was a bad sign. Jumping from the floppy disk in the A: drive to the hard disk on the C: drive was a big step, but going from the C: drive to another partition on that same drive, or to a networked drive on another computer altogether, set the stage for the disasters we encounter far too frequently today.

The Internet, and universal e-mail, have made virus distribution almost too easy. Chapter 8, "How Viruses Are Spread," is filled with examples of the "improvements" made possible by today's connected environment, but a few of them are covered here.

## The Address Book as a distribution method

One major step in virus distribution took place with the discovery of Address Books as a source of e-mail addresses to receive a virus. That quickly became the preferred method of spreading a virus; in response, some e-mail users quit using their Address Book in a vain attempt to protect their correspondents from viruses. Scrapping this useful tool meant a lot more work for senders of e-mail, but it seemed worth the effort to some users.

Unfortunately, the newer viruses use more sophisticated techniques to find e-mail addresses on an infected system. Instead of, or sometimes in addition to, looking for an Address Book, these viruses will scan all of the e-mail messages and other files on the infected system, looking for individual e-mail addresses.

That's a pretty easy task to accomplish, looking for the @ character in an e-mail message and seeing if that symbol is followed by something that has the format of a Web address, and the symbol is preceded by a possible user name. If so, that e-mail address is added to the list of targets for the subject virus.

Especially if you have e-mail correspondents who send messages to multiple recipients, and list all of those addresses in the To: or the Cc: field of the message, all of those addresses are susceptible to this means of attack. That's why it's critically important that any broadcast e-mail messages have the addressees placed in the Bcc: field instead, so that those addresses do not show up on the recipient computers.

Another example of a virus distribution technique that was innovative when first introduced was the idea of using an e-mail attachment to spread the virus. The text of the e-mail message might direct the recipient to open the attachment and play a game, take a quiz, or see a joke or a pornographic picture. Of course, the actual effect of the attachment was to infect the computer with the virus.

## Newer distribution methods have become more sophisticated

Realizing that computer users were becoming wise to the ways of virus distribution, the virus writers have sought out new ways to encourage unsuspecting recipients to open the virus attachment. One fairly creative approach was used by the "My Party" virus, which urged the recipient to click on the attachment to go to the sender's Web site.

There were two problems here. The first was that the name of the attachment, which had a suffix of .com, was identified as a Web site; in fact, it was actually an executable file. Many users don't realize that a file with a .com extension is an executable program, the same as a file with a .exe extension.

The other problem with this message was that it appeared to come from someone known to the recipient. Because of that familiarity, the recipient was likely to follow the instructions without questioning the logic of doing so. This is another technique that has become the standard approach for most modern viruses. It is known as "spoofing" the sender's address, which is distressingly easy for anyone with reasonable technical skills to accomplish.

A later example of the virus writers' learning curve illustrates the danger of outdated knowledge on the subject. This technique was first used successfully on a massive basis with the Nimda virus. It is the approach of including executable program code in an e-mail message that will infect the target system. In other words, it's no longer necessary to open an attachment in order to become infected by a virus that uses this technique.

## Now, some viruses find your computer without your help

As of this writing, the latest giant step forward in virus distribution is the technique that was first widely exploited by the Blaster worm. As discussed earlier, this worm spread randomly to computer addresses generated by the worm itself. It did not come through an e-mail message or any other means that was initiated by the computer user.

Table 4.1 lists 30 of the most widespread viruses, including some that may have infected your computer systems. These aren't necessarily the "30 worst" examples, but they were some of the most commonly occurring, most damaging, or were responsible for introducing some new technique that has since become a staple of the virus writer's trade.

This list, given in alphabetical order, has changed numerous times since the author first created it. This is just one person's opinion of the most significant virus threats over the years, and the list is always subject to change. How many of these names do you recognize?

**Table 4.1  Top 30 Viruses**

| | |
|---|---|
| • Anna Kournikova | • Melissa |
| • Back Orifice | • Michelangelo |
| • Badtrans | • MyDoom |
| • Bagle / Beagle | • MyParty |
| • Blaster / Lovsan | • NetSky |
| • Bugbear | • Nimda |
| • CIH (Chernobyl) | • Opaserv |
| • Code Red | • PrettyPark |
| • Funlove | • Sapphire / Slammer |
| • Hybris (Snow White) | • Sasser |
| • Iloveyou (Love Letter) | • Scob / Download.Ject |
| • Kak | • Sircam |
| • Klez / Elkern | • Sobig.A through Sobig.F |
| • Lovgate | • Swen-A |
| • Magistr | • Welchia |

You'll notice that some of these viruses / worms have multiple names. The reason for this ambiguity is the practice of the different AV software vendors assigning names to the various pieces of malware as they identify them. Especially if several vendors discover a new virus at about the same time, different names may be used to define the same offender.

There is actually a convention that defines how viruses are to be named, but many of the AV software vendors have added their own variations to that specification. If you'd like to see the original recommendations, adopted by the Computer Antivirus Research Organization (CARO) in 1991, they can be found on the Internet in a number of different locations.

Although CARO itself does not seem to have a readily accessible Web site, a search on any major search engine will reveal abundant references for finding the original specification. When you consider the wholesale changes in the virus landscape since 1991, it's easy to understand why the AV software companies have added their own customization.

If you're investigating a specific virus or worm, the logical place to look for further information is the Web site provided by the vendor of the AV software you are using on that computer. Each vendor's description of a specific virus usually references the other names assigned to this threat by the other major AV software vendors.

# Chapter 5
## Who Writes Viruses, and Why?

One question that invariably arises when discussing viruses is, "Who produces viruses, and why do they do it?" or words to that effect. While the answer to this question was pretty simple and straightforward a few years ago, it has recently become a far more complex issue.

## High-Tech Vandals

The original purpose of computer viruses was vandalism, pure and simple. The virus writers chose to infect your computer, instead of throwing a brick through your window. They could write their viruses any time of day or night, in the comfort of their own home, with little likelihood of being caught in the act.

In addition to the satisfaction the virus writer derived from seeing (or reading about) the results of his (almost all virus writers are male) mischief, there was a bonus payoff from those efforts. A successful virus attack proved that the writer possessed some technical skills, beyond the abilities of "average" people.

## The Profit Motive

There have been some major changes in the rationale for producing viruses in the past few years, though. For many virus writers today, the payoff is monetary. There are several ways a successful virus attack can generate considerable revenue for the perpetrator.

## Harvesting and Selling E-mail Addresses

The most profitable return from a virus, with the lowest level of risk, comes from harvesting e-mail addresses from infected computers and selling those addresses to spammers. Even if the addresses are sold for pennies apiece, an effective virus could easily collect millions of e-mail addresses, and sell each one to multiple spammers.

## Turning Infected Computers Into Zombies

One of the fastest-growing ways virus writers are realizing a profit from their mischief is in turning infected computers into zombies. When a virus has infected a large number of computers, these computers can be coordinated into a widespread network capable of doing the bidding of the virus writer.

Such a network of zombie computers can be used to broadcast spam e-mail messages and phishing scams, for a price. In the process, they will also attempt to spread to additional computers and thus increase the size (and value) of the zombie network.

According to one recent estimate by a large e-mailer, nearly 40% of all spam messages sent today are originating from zombie networks. And most of the owners of these infected computers have no idea their computer is being used in such a distasteful way.

A recent posting on an Internet listserv for spammers gives an example of the value of such zombie networks. The asking price for the use of a network of some 20,000 computers ranges from $2,000 to $3,000.

## Distributed Denial-of-Service (DDoS) Attacks

Another potentially profitable use of zombie networks is to unleash a Distributed Denial-of-Service attack against a targeted Web site. In a DDoS attack, zombie networks flood the Web site with thousands of data requests simultaneously. With a large enough network of zombie computers, each sending hundreds of requests per second, it is possible to overwhelm the servers of any business, organization, or government agency.

Initial DDoS attacks were aimed at businesses or government agencies who were perceived to have behaved badly, or whose purpose was considered unjust by the virus creators. Major targets included the Department of Defense, Microsoft, and the Santa Cruz Operation (developer of SCO Unix). There is usually no profit motive behind this type of DDoS attack.

On the other hand, some modern virus writers use the threat of such an attack to extort protection money from businesses who fear the thought of their Web site being unavailable for any significant length of time. These cyber-crooks have updated one of the old reliable forms of criminal activity to fit the way business is transacted in the 21st century.

## Identity Theft

A source of potentially much greater income than selling harvested e-mail addresses, but with a considerably higher degree of risk, is to have the virus scan the infected computers for financial and identity information, and resell that information to criminals, including identity thieves.

A virus with this intent could easily be programmed to search the entire hard drive of an infected computer, looking for credit card numbers, other account numbers, Social Security Numbers, birth dates, and other personal identity information. In the corporate environment, these viruses will be looking for Logon IDs and Passwords. Any of this data is very much in demand by the criminal element.

## Cyber-Terrorism

So, there's now a strong economic reward for successful virus writers. And there's another reason for virus writers to pursue this career path: since September 11, 2001, we need to consider the possibility of viruses being used as a terrorist tool.

Regardless of any political, social, or religious justification, the very act of producing a computer virus and releasing it into the wild is increasingly being regarded as an act of cyber-terrorism. In the near future, we are likely to see new laws that treat virus writers and hackers more as terrorists than as vandals.

## Psychological Profile

Since we've just mentioned virus writers and hackers in the same paragraph, it's important to understand the difference between the two categories of troublemakers. It's not always a clear-cut distinction, because there is some overlap between the two groups.

We'll use the term hackers to represent those people who use their technical skills to break into networks. They are generally older than virus writers, and more advanced technologically. By definition, hackers don't necessarily have criminal intent when they find a way into someone else's computer.

The primary motivation for hackers, especially those who use their hacking skills for criminal purposes, is the feeling of power. They are in control of the systems they commandeer, and from there they can do as they please with the "hacked" system. It looks like a big game to them, and they've won. They solved the puzzle.

Virus writers, on the other hand, usually have simpler motivations, and shorter careers in their field of malware. They are generally younger, and many are still in school. Many of them fit the stereotype of the introverted geek who lacks a social life, and produce viruses to prove their value as a person.

*(Note that this is not intended as a complete psychological treatise, and references will be given later in this chapter to sites that delve into more of the personality traits of virus writers and hackers!)*

While virus writers are not necessarily great programmers, they are usually of above-average intelligence. Becoming a programmer in the first place requires a fairly high level of intelligence, but virus writers typically are not at the head of their class.

That said, the best virus writers truly are talented. The viruses that have spread the most destruction, and replicated most prolifically, were invariably produced by programmers with a high level of skill.

## Sharing the Knowledge

Another reason for the increasingly virulent spread of viruses is the fact that the best virus writers learn from one another. When a new virus comes out, with a new payload or distribution method, that technique will be incorporated in future viruses, as each virus writer adds his own new twists and turns to the next generation of viruses.

As mentioned earlier, the virus producers have their own community, complete with Web sites, chat rooms, newsletters, and even face-to-face conventions. The most dedicated members of this community are always on the lookout to exchange ideas with their peers for the next great virus attack.

## A Little Bit of Good News

There is actually some good news, though, about the psychological profile of virus writers. Very few of them make a career of this type of activity. Some graduate to hacking for pay, but many just grow bored with the "game" and move on to a different form of diversion or challenge.

Many virus writers, especially the younger ones, truly don't realize or comprehend the extent of damage their efforts can cause. Many of them have no concept of moral or ethical behavior, especially in relationship to the world of business, computers and the Internet. Some virus researchers have suggested that teaching ethical behavior to children would have a significant effect on reducing the spread of viruses.

## What About Punishment?

So, what about punishment? When a virus writer is caught, what happens to him? Unfortunately, we don't have many opportunities to find out – very few virus writers are ever identified and apprehended.

The structure of the Internet and the e-mail system that most of us use makes it extremely easy for a virus writer to remain anonymous. It's a rare event when the originator of a virus is uncovered as a result of great police work. From a technological standpoint, it's very difficult to follow the trail of a virus infection back to its original source.

In almost every case of a virus writer being apprehended, it's because he left clues to his identity in the virus itself, or bragged about his success to the wrong person. It's a pretty safe bet that law enforcement agencies are monitoring some of the Web sites and chat rooms used by these people, so every now and then the "good guys" get a break.

But even when the offender has been identified, the game may not be over. One reason is that many viruses originate outside of the United States, and this activity is not illegal in most foreign countries. Even in the United States, there is so much variation in the laws from one state to another that it may be impractical to prosecute a confessed virus writer.

As state and federal lawmakers become more aware of the damage that can be caused by virus writers and hackers, we can expect to see more laws enacted to deal with this new age of criminal activity. Especially if these activities are classified as terrorism, it should be easier to have new laws passed to deal with this breed of criminal.

If you're interested in learning more about the psychological makeup of virus writers and hackers, there are many sources on the Internet where you can find that information. Some of the ideas presented in this chapter were developed from two articles by Monte Enbysk, on Microsoft's bCentral Web site, as follows:

- *7 things to know about virus writers*, at http://www.bcentral.com/articles/enbysk/160.asp

- *Hacking into the mind of a hacker*, at http://www.bcentral.com/articles/enbysk/164.asp

Another valuable reference came from Susan Gordon, at www.badguys.org.

## Who Doesn't Write Viruses

As there is a fair degree of suspicion among computer users on this subject, it may also be helpful to talk about who doesn't introduce these viruses to the world. That would be the anti-virus software vendors themselves.

While these vendors obviously have a vested interest in the spread of viruses, it would be economic suicide for their business if any of them were to deliberately introduce a virus into the wild. If it could ever be proven that an AV software vendor was the original source of a widespread virus attack, it's difficult to even imagine the consequences they would suffer.

If you only consider the liability of such a company in terms of dollars, that figure would certainly be measured in billions or tens of billions. That factor in itself would put the company out of business, and probably bankrupt the officers of the corporation as well.

As if that weren't enough of a potential downside to discourage such an activity, consider the political fallout. Various governmental agencies and elected officials would find such a company an irresistible target for new regulations, fines, criminal prosecution, and public humiliation. What Senator or Representative could resist the temptation to demonstrate their concern for the "little people" against a big, evil corporation that has deliberately caused such harm?

So no, you don't need to worry about Symantec, or McAfee, or any of the other major AV software companies introducing new viruses to a vulnerable public. There's plenty of this activity taking place, without these vendors having to generate any more malware.

## Inside the AV Labs

That's not to say that these companies are not being proactive in their efforts to protect us from viruses. They are always looking for new methods the virus writers could use to exploit another vulnerability of the Operating System, the network environment, or a particular Web browser or e-mail program. Once these vulnerabilities have been identified, the vendors can then develop a "fix" that will protect their clients' computers from such an attack.

But any of these new techniques developed in-house are kept there, in the "zoo." Just like the animals in a zoo, the viruses contained in the in-house zoo can't cause any harm to the outside world. When a virus has been released to general distribution, it is referred to as being "in the wild." That's when it can start causing trouble.

One reason many people suspect the AV software vendors of being responsible for the release of new viruses is the speed with which they release a cure for newly discovered viruses. Instead of castigating these software companies for this responsiveness, we truly owe them a debt of gratitude for paying such close attention to what is going on in the world of everyday users, and the software that we depend on.

Within a few hours of a new virus outbreak, most of the major AV software vendors will have at least preliminary information on their Web site about this latest offender. They may not have a software removal tool right away, but usually by the end of the day there will be the initial release of such a tool. Over the following hours and days, the tool may be updated and improved numerous times as the vendor learns more about the details of the virus and the damage it inflicts. A typical example of this diligence was the reaction to the Blaster worm. Symantec offered their first removal tool, Version 1.0.0, the day the worm was first detected. Within two days, the tool had been updated four times, to Version 1.0.4.

## What About Microsoft?

Another software vendor who is frequently vilified by computer users is Microsoft, for producing Operating Systems that are vulnerable to these attacks. The criticisms fall into two general categories, both of which are understandable on the surface.

The most general complaint is the fact that the various versions of Windows are susceptible to infection by viruses, worms, Trojan horses, and other forms of malware. But when you consider this argument from Microsoft's perspective, these vulnerabilities are a natural consequence of the flexibility and openness of their Operating Systems.

One of the main reasons for the success of the Windows platform is the ease of developing software that runs successfully in this environment. Microsoft publishes the specifications for software interfaces, and does everything reasonably possible to encourage software vendors to develop applications that are compatible with the look and feel of Windows.

From the user's standpoint, the Windows Operating System and applications are written to be as "user-friendly" as possible, with standardized, consistent dialog boxes and procedures to follow across most applications. Microsoft places much more emphasis on ease of use than on throwing up roadblocks to keep the "bad guys" out.

Any form of security is a trade-off between flexibility, compatibility, and ease of use at one end of the scale, and protection against threats at the other end. By definition, the more secure any software is, the more difficult it will be to use, and the more limited will be its options in terms of support for additional hardware and software applications.

The other general criticism of Microsoft is the fact that no current version of Windows includes virus prevention or detection. Once upon a time, in the era of Windows 3.x, anti-virus software was included in the Operating System. That was before third-party software vendors rose to prominence selling AV software.

At that time in Microsoft's life, the Justice Department hadn't become involved in the content of the software the company was selling. In the intervening years, each new version of Windows included features and capabilities that had formerly been available only through third-party software vendors.

Responding to objections from these vendors, the government has put Microsoft in the position of not trying to include everything in their software. Until recently, it appeared that the path of least resistance for Microsoft would be to stay out of the AV software business for the time being.

As of mid-2005, it appears that Microsoft is on the verge of reversing that position. With the increased spread of viruses and the rising rate of infection, Microsoft has become more concerned about security issues as they affect the Windows environment.

The company has announced tentative plans to offer an AV software product of its own in the near future. It is not clear whether this software will become a standard feature of the Windows Operating Systems or a separate stand-alone product. Nor has any pricing information been forthcoming.

# Chapter 6
## The Importance of Backups

From the time we started using our first computer, we've all been told the importance of backups. We all know that we need to have additional copies of our important data files, in case something happens to the original versions of those files.

## Why Make Backups?

In the early days of the computer industry, the reason for the emphasis on backups was obvious. The computer hardware was sometimes unreliable, and it was only prudent to assume that the hard drive of your computer would fail, sooner rather than later.

As computer hardware has evolved, most users have come to depend upon the reliability of their systems. Actual failures of hard drives are so rare on modern computer systems that many users have been lulled into a false sense of security and believe that data backups are no longer necessary.

With the proliferation of viruses in today's computing environment, though, there's a renewed need to back up your data on a regular basis. Even if your computer never suffers a hardware failure, a virus infection could be every bit as destructive to your critical data. If you want to be able to recover from the damage caused by a virus, it is vital that you back up your data on a regular schedule.

## When and How to Back Up

Among home computer users, it is rare to find backups being performed on a regular basis, if at all. In small to mid-sized businesses, there are usually some backups being made of the most important data files, but these organizations rarely follow procedures that would allow for recovery from a worst-case scenario.

There are a number of factors that need to be considered when defining your backup methods, media, and procedures. This chapter will discuss these variables in some detail.

## 1. The Backup Method

The first consideration is which backup method to use. There are three general types of backup, and each is appropriate at different times in the backup cycle. These categories include Image Backups, Full Data Backups, and Incremental Backups.

Image backups are intended to save an image of the entire hard drive, to allow for recovery in the event of a total system failure or hard drive replacement. This is the largest and most time-consuming form of backup procedure, but it is recommended that you have at least one image backup of your full system.

Full data backups consist of making copies of all of your data files, in a manner that will allow you to restore those data files to a different computer. You may also use these backups to restore the files to the same computer in case of emergency, whether that be the result of a hardware failure, inadvertent erasure, or corruption of some of these data files. By definition, individual files may be restored from a full data backup set.

Incremental backups are interim backup procedures, performed between times of full data backups or image backups. Incremental backups make copies of only the data that has changed since the last backup was performed; as a result, the time and media space required by incremental backups is only a small fraction of that used by the other methods.

The disadvantage of incremental backups is that you must always maintain the prior backup media upon which the incremental backup is based. If you're doing a full data backup weekly, and incremental backups daily, you'll need to save every day's incremental backup media until the next full data backup is produced.

## 2. The Backup Media

The second consideration in your backup routine is the type of media to use. There is a wide range of choices available, each with its own advantages and disadvantages. These are the categories of devices and their associated media to consider for this critical task:

- Floppy disks
- Zip or Jaz cartridges
- CD-R or CD-RW disks
- DVD-R or DVD-RW disks
- Magnetic tapes
- Second hard drive
- Network hard drive
- External hard drive
- Online backup services

There are other backup media you may want to consider, which are not yet in sufficiently widespread use to be included in this evaluation. An example would be removable USB Flash Memory drives; these go by names such as Jump drives, Keychain drives, Micro Mini drives (by Iomega), Thumb drives, or Pen drives (in the U.K.).

Here are some of the factors that come into play when deciding which medium is the appropriate choice for your backups:

- Capacity of media
- Backup/Restore Speed
- Compatibility with other computers
- Reliability of device/media
- Media cost
- Unattended backups
- Ability to store off-site

Here are the pros and cons of each backup medium, with respect to the factors listed above:

## Floppy Disks

3½" floppy disks have the advantage of being ubiquitous, as a standard component of virtually every personal computer produced since 1987. Some of the newest computers have made a floppy drive an optional component, and some laptop computers may require an external floppy drive, but every computer has the ability to support a 3½" floppy drive. Another benefit of floppy disks is compatibility – any modern diskette drive can read a floppy disk produced on any other computer, assuming that the diskette is formatted to store 1.44 MB of data.

The primary disadvantage of floppy disks, of course, is their limited capacity. When these drives were first introduced, it was practical to back up an entire hard drive on a few floppy disks. Today, there are many individual files that won't even come close to fitting on a floppy diskette. Also, the speed of recording to a floppy disk is very slow.

Notice that this discussion is confined to 3½" drives. In case you still have a computer old enough to include a 5¼" floppy drive, don't even think of backing up any important data to those diskettes!

## Zip and Jaz Disks

Zip disks offer a higher capacity and faster data transfer than floppy disks, but at a much higher media cost. As these drives are not found on most computers, the issue of compatibility may prevent restoring the backed-up data on a different computer.

The Jaz cartridge provides even higher capacity than Zip disks, and a much faster rate of data transfer, but the media cost is very high. Further, these drives were never produced in the quantities of other backup devices, so it may be difficult to restore data from a Jaz cartridge to a different computer.

## CD-R and CD-RW Disks

CD-R (Recordable) disks have become the most popular backup medium in recent years, with good reason. They offer high capacity (approximately 600 Megabytes), reasonable speed, and very low media cost. There is some degree of incompatibility with older CD-ROM drives, but this is rarely an issue.

The related CD-RW (ReWritable) disks, while offering the advantage of reusability, are saddled with too many potential problems to be a prudent backup medium. The cost of blank CD-RW disks, which is much higher than that of CD-R disks, is supposedly justified by their rewritability.

In practice, though, rewriting a file on a CD-RW disk may be problematic. In too many cases, a Rewrite has appeared to be done properly, when in fact the old version of the file has been left intact, and the newer version has been lost. Also, CD-ROM drives that are more than a few years old will be unable to read CD-RW media successfully.

In light of these potential problems, CD-RW disks are not recommended as a backup medium for your important data files. In a rare turn of events, even the manufacturers of these drives are now discouraging use of CD-RW disks for data backups.

## DVD-R and DVD-RW Disks

As the "big brother" of CD-ROM disks, DVD disks may be a suitable backup medium. The capacity of these disks ranges from roughly eight to fourteen times that of a CD-ROM.

One of the major issues with recordable DVD media today is the wide range of methods used by different drives. There is DVD-R, DVD+R, DVD-RW, DVD+RW, and DVD-RAM. Until a unified standard emerges, compatibility is an important consideration in deciding whether to use this medium for backups.

A related issue is the capacity of the drive, and the media it will accommodate. While the original DVD disks would hold approximately 4.7 Gigabytes of data, the current technology uses two layers of recording surface on the disk. This technique allows the disk to contain roughly 8.5 Gigabytes.

## Magnetic Tapes

Magnetic tapes have been the preferred backup medium by many people for quite a few years. They are especially favored by IT Departments and individuals with experience on the mainframe side of computers. But times have changed since these preferences were formed, and magnetic tapes are rarely the backup medium of choice today.

The advantage of magnetic tape has always been its high capacity. If you need a removable medium that will store tens of gigabytes of data, then you may have no other choice but tape. But the high cost of media, serious compatibility and reliability issues, and the long time required to do a backup or restore make it difficult to recommend this medium for most users.

## Second Hard Drive

In many ways the best backup medium is a second hard drive. This will produce the fastest backups and restores, very high capacity, and excellent reliability. There are three different forms of hard drive backup that you may want to consider, each with its own benefits and drawbacks.

One method is to back up to a second hard drive in the same computer case that houses the primary hard drive. This is the simplest, fastest, "cleanest" and least expensive way of achieving this goal, but it doesn't give you the option of taking the backup media off-site for secure storage.

A second possibility is to back up to a network hard drive, housed in a server or another computer on the network. The data transfer is considerably slower across the network than it would be with a locally attached hard drive, but is still very fast. This approach does offer the added benefit of the backup being off-site, or at least in a different "box."

The third option for using a hard drive as a backup device is to use an external hard drive for the purpose. If connected via a USB 2.0 or IEEE 1394 (FireWire) connection, these drives will transfer data at approximately half the speed of a locally installed hard drive. This is several times faster than you are likely to achieve on a network drive.

As an external device, this hard drive can be stored off-site for maximum security. Since it does not contain removable media, the media cost is the full cost of the drive itself. This represents the most expensive form of backup, but you may very well decide the cost is justified by the benefits it offers.

## Online Backup Services

The final backup option to consider is online backup services. These backups are done over the Internet, to a secure location that typically offers multiple lcvcls of redundancy.  These services let you choose how much data you want to back up, how frequently it will be done, and various other options, depending upon the provider.

The benefits of online backup include their unlimited capacity, the flexibility they give you in scheduling the size and frequency of backups, and the absence of any hardware or media cost to perform the backups.

On the downside, the monthly cost of using such a service could actually make this the most expensive backup method for you.  Also, the speed of backups and restores will depend upon your connection to the Internet.  This is probably not a practical backup method to employ if you connect to the Internet via a dial-up modem.

Table 6.1 summarizes the advantages and disadvantages of each of these media choices.

### Table 6.1 Advantages and Disadvantages of Backup Media

| Medium | Capacity | Speed | Compatibility | Reliability | Off Site | Unattended | Media Cost |
|---|---|---|---|---|---|---|---|
| Floppy Disks | Low | Slow | 100% | High | Yes | No | Low |
| Zip Disks | Moderate to High | Moderate | 100% | Very High | Yes | No | High |
| Jaz Cartridges | High | Moderate | 100% | Very High | Yes | No | Very High |
| CD-R Disks | High | Moderate | High | High | Yes | No | Low |
| CD-RW Disks | High | Moderate | Moderate | Moderate | Yes | No | High |
| Recordable DVD (Multiple formats) | Higher | Moderate | Varies | Moderate | Yes | No | Moderate |
| Magnetic Tapes | Very High | Moderate | Problematic | Problematic | Yes | Maybe | High |
| 2nd Hard Drive | Very High | Fastest | 100% | Very High | No | Yes | N/A |
| Network Drive | Very High | Fast | 100% | Very High | Maybe | Yes | N/A |
| External Hard Drive | Very High | 2nd Fastest | 100% | Very High | Yes | Yes | N/A |
| Online Service | Very High | Slow | 100% | Very High | Yes | Yes | Monthly |

## 3. The Backup Software

Once you've decided on the backup medium you'll be using, the third consideration is the software you'll use to make the backups. There are several categories to consider here.

### Backup Software Bundled With Hardware

When you buy a hardware device that is intended to be used for backups, it will probably include some software to make the backup procedure easier and more automatic for you. Devices such as CD-RW drives, Iomega Zip drives, and external hard drives will typically come bundled with some backup software.

In many cases, the software included with the hardware is a stripped-down, or "lite" version of a more powerful product from the software vendor. Depending upon your needs, you may want to upgrade to the full version of the backup software package. Such an upgrade is usually offered at a substantial discount from the full product price.

### Other Backup Software

There are other backup software products you may want to consider buying, especially if you choose to make image backups of your hard drive. Products such as Ghost (from Symantec) and DriveImage (from PowerQuest) are designed to make a full image copy of your hard drive. If you replace the hard drive in that system, or if you have multiple computers that need the exact same configuration, one of these programs can save you a lot of repetitive manual effort.

Of course, your Operating System may include a backup utility that will meet all of your needs. Some versions of Windows include a backup program, while others don't. But all of the Windows versions give you the ability to copy files manually.

In most cases, if you want a simple backup procedure that doesn't require a separate utility program, you can use Windows Explorer. Simply Copy the files or folders you want to back up, and Paste them into the desired destination. Although it's not elegant, this procedure serves the purpose and works under any version of Windows.

## 4A. What (Not) To Back Up

The fourth consideration in backups is deciding what will be backed up. If you've already decided to make an Image Backup every time, you may skip the next few paragraphs. But if you need to make the most effective use of your time and minimize your cost of backup media, you'll want to consider your options.

As a general statement, there's no point in making backup copies of the programs that are installed on your computer, other than as a part of a full image backup. In the case of a total hardware failure or hard drive replacement, copying individual programs onto a new hard drive will rarely produce successful results.

The reason those programs are unlikely to work when copied onto a new hard drive relates to the way Windows programs are installed. In the original installation procedure, most of the program components are copied into a folder on the hard drive, typically under C:\Program Files\Application Name. If you tried to make a backup copy of the program, that's the folder you would normally copy.

But there's much more to the program installation procedure than that. In addition to the application folder, some files may be copied into the \Windows folder, or \Windows\System, or other system folders. You have no easy way of knowing where these additional files are located, how many there are, or their file names.

Also, the installation program probably makes numerous changes to the Windows Registry. This is an enormous and mysterious database that contains everything the Operating System knows about its environment. That definitely includes information about all the programs that are installed on the computer.

If you copy a program to a new hard drive but don't make the necessary changes in the Registry, you won't be able to run the program. Unless Windows (of any version) sees the information it needs in the Registry, it won't know that the program exists on that computer, much less how to run it.

## 4B. What To Back Up

So, that's what not to back up. Just plan on reinstalling all of your programs when you replace a hard drive or upgrade to a new computer. Which leads to the question, what do you need to back up?

Here's the short answer: just your data files. The longer answer gets into the definition of your data files. Here are the general categories you want to be sure are always included in any regular backup:

- Documents, templates, and forms you have created
- Data files from any accounting, database, or other applications
- Contact management and schedule information
- E-mail folders and Address Books
- Internet Browser Favorites or Bookmarks

In most cases, you will know where these files are stored and how to include them in your backup routine. There are several of these items that may require special treatment, though, so here are some tips to help you find what you need.

Rather than looking for the folder and/or file that contains your Address Book, the safest way to back up that data is by using the Export function of your e-mail program. Most Address Books of reasonable size will easily fit on a single floppy disk, so you may want to periodically export your Address Book to a floppy disk and store it in a safe place.

Just as you use the Export function of your e-mail program to back up your Address Book, you'll probably want to use the Export function of your Internet Browser to save your Favorites or Bookmarks. In most Browsers, simply click on File and choose Export, then select Favorites or Bookmarks. These will almost certainly fit on a single floppy disk, which you can then store in a safe place.

### Finding Your Address Book

If you really want to find the actual Address Book file on your hard drive, Microsoft Outlook stores these entries in the .pst file. By default, the full file name is Outlook.pst, but yours may be somewhat different. If you don't see a file by that name, a Search or Find for *.pst should reveal its location and exact file name.

Outlook Express (OE) uses a separate file for the Address Book, with a File Type, or extension, of .wab. By default, the full file name is Computername. wab. Similar to the procedure described above for Outlook, you can find an elusive OE Address Book by doing a Search or Find on *.wab and seeing its full name and the folder in which it is found.

### Finding Your E-Mail

Your actual e-mail messages may be similarly difficult to find, so here are some clues to help you locate them. In Outlook, everything is stored in the single .pst file where you found your Address Book. If you back up that file, you'll be saving your Address Book, Schedule, and all your e-mail folders.

By the same token, if anything happens to that file, you've lost all of this information. That's one more example of why backups can be so important!

In Outlook Express, each e-mail folder you have defined becomes a .dbx file. The default location of these folders is at least six levels deep, if you're looking for it in Windows Explorer, so here's the simple way to locate your e-mail folders in Outlook Express.

In OE, click on Tools, then choose Options... On the Maintenance tab, click on Store Folder... That reveals the location of your e-mail folders and lets you change it if necessary. For example, you may want to change this entry to point to a previous set of e-mail folders, or possibly those of another user.

If you're using an e-mail program other than Microsoft Outlook or Outlook Express, you may need to do some digging in order to find the location of your e-mail messages. One technique that will usually work is to do a search for a file named inbox.*. Most e-mail programs use a file by that name, with varying file types, or extensions. When you locate a file by that name, the folder in which it is stored will probably contain all of your saved e-mail messages.

### 5A. How Often Should You Back Up?

With all this information in hand, you can include those specific files and folders in any backup you perform. That brings us to the fifth and final consideration in defining your backup procedures – how often to perform backups and how long to retain them.

The answers to both those questions, of course, are "it depends." Any backup routine is a trade-off of the time it takes to make the backups versus the time that would be lost if you had to recreate or reenter the lost data. For most individual users, the balance comes at weekly backups. You may want to perform backups daily, especially if a large amount of data is entered or changed on your computer every day.

Regardless of your backup cycle, it is critically important that you cycle your backup media in such a way that you can always restore the data to its current state as of the end of the previous week, month, quarter, and year. For most users, this concept represents a marked departure from the way they have been backing up their data thus far.

## 5B. How Long Should You Retain the Backups?

The temptation is to keep reusing the same backup media, whether that be magnetic tape, Zip disk, or even floppy diskettes. This is especially true in the case of expensive storage media, such as magnetic tapes. But following this "path of least resistance" defeats much of the purpose of backups in the first place.

The potential problem is that, in the case of virus infection or otherwise corrupted data files, the damage may not be apparent for some time after it first occurs. Especially in the case of viruses, your computer could have been infected for months before any symptoms become obvious.

If your only backup in this situation is from last week, or from yesterday, you will not be able to restore those infected files from a time before the damage occurred. In other words, you may as well have no backup at all.

Before you start mentally calculating the cost of 52 magnetic tapes, or Zip disks, or other expensive media, be aware that you won't need nearly that many. By properly cycling your media, you can achieve the desired objective with as few as 7 storage media per year.

Table 6.2 illustrates a sample media rotation that will always give you the ability to restore your backed-up data to its condition as of the end of the previous week, month, quarter and year, while investing in only 7 backup media. You may want to modify this scheme if you prefer to keep every month's backup for a year, or any other variation that will let you sleep more soundly at night.

This rotation cycle makes several assumptions, which you may adjust to fit your circumstances or preferences:

- You have a full data backup prior to Week 1 of this schedule.
- You don't need to make daily backups.
- You don't plan to keep every month's backup for a year.
- The first month of the cycle includes five weeks, followed by two months of four weeks each.

The way this table is designed to be used, each backup medium (tape, Zip disk, etc.) is assigned a letter, ranging from A through G. Each weekly backup will be kept for 4 or 5 weeks; each monthly backup will be kept for 13 weeks; and each quarterly backup will be kept for 26 weeks.

Note that you can use this same approach with a hard drive, whether it be internal, external, or a network drive. Simply define folders named "Backup Cycle A" through "Backup Cycle G," or any other names you choose.

## Table 6.2 – Backup Media Rotation

| Week | Week | Month | Quarter | Year | Week | Week | Month | Quarter | Year |
|------|------|-------|---------|------|------|------|-------|---------|------|
| 1 | A | | | | 27 | A | | | |
| 2 | B | | | | 28 | B | | | |
| 3 | C | | | | 29 | C | | | |
| 4 | D | | | | 30 | H | | | |
| 5 | E | E | | | 31 | E | E | | |
| 6 | A | | | | 32 | A | | | |
| 7 | B | | | | 33 | B | | | |
| 8 | C | | | | 34 | C | | | |
| 9 | D | D | | | 35 | D | D | | |
| 10 | A | | | | 36 | A | | | |
| 11 | B | | | | 37 | B | | | |
| 12 | C | | | | 38 | C | | | |
| 13 | F | F | F | | 39 | F | F | F | |
| 14 | A | | | | 40 | A | | | |
| 15 | B | | | | 41 | B | | | |
| 16 | C | | | | 42 | C | | | |
| 17 | G | | | | 43 | G | | | |
| 18 | E | E | | | 44 | E | E | | |
| 19 | A | | | | 45 | A | | | |
| 20 | B | | | | 46 | B | | | |
| 21 | C | | | | 47 | C | | | |
| 22 | D | D | | | 48 | D | D. | | |
| 23 | A | | | | 49 | A | | | |
| 24 | B | | | | 50 | B | | | |
| 25 | C | | | | 51 | C | | | |
| 26 | G | G | G | | 52 | G | G | G | G |

One final point on backups – regardless of the method you use to create your backups, always test it to be sure the procedure you're following, the software, the backup device, and the storage medium are actually producing a usable backup before you need it. There are far too many horror stories of backups that were done faithfully, but only when there was a need to restore the data was it discovered that the backup was unusable.

# Chapter 7
## Kinds of Damage Viruses May Cause

By definition, a computer virus doesn't necessarily cause any damage to the computers it infects. If a program replicates itself and spreads from one computer to another, it meets the definition of a virus.

While any virus has the potential to damage the computers it infects, the most destructive category of virus is frequently the worm. In this chapter we'll cover some of the kinds of damage that may be the result of a virus/worm infection.

### Infecting Files

Most viruses will, at a minimum, infect additional files on the infected computer. In addition to the hard drive, the virus may spread to floppy diskettes, other backup media, and possibly across the Local Area Network or the Internet. Programs and data files in all of these locations could be the subject of a second-generation virus infection.

### Harvesting E-Mail Addresses

Even if a virus doesn't cause any direct damage to the infected computer, it may exploit that computer in several ways that could cause indirect damage. Most viruses will scan their infected hosts looking for e-mail addresses, and then send themselves to those addresses. Some will also randomly select a file on the infected computer, infect that file with the virus, and forward it to the e-mail addresses the virus found there.

In addition to the e-mail messages the virus sends from the infected computer to spread the virus, it is likely that those addresses will also be used to make a profit for the virus writer. He can achieve this objective by selling the harvested e-mail addresses to spammers. Even if the selling price per address is extremely low, most successful viruses can accumulate thousands of addresses and sell them to multiple buyers.

## Leaving a "Back Door" Open

Another variation on the theme of forwarding your data files is a technique that is installed through a "back door" routine included in some viruses. This vulnerability may be used to have the virus send specific files or data found on your computer to the author of the virus, or to someone else who has paid to receive that information.

If the virus leaves such a "back door" open, there is virtually no limit to the damage or invasion of privacy the virus writer could cause. He could delete files, cause programs to run, restrict programs from being able to run, make changes to your computer's Registry, or duplicate anything else you can do when you're sitting at that computer.

Another possible result of a "back door" is a keystroke recorder, or key logger. These programs keep a record of every key you type on your keyboard, and periodically send that file to the author of the virus. By seeing the actual keys you pressed, the hacker can recognize account numbers, Logon IDs and Passwords, and other sensitive information that could be valuable keys to identity theft.

## Deleting or Corrupting Files

Moving on to more obviously destructive behavior that may be caused by a virus, perhaps the most common example would be deleting or corrupting files on the infected computer. There are several broad categories of files that may be targeted:

- System files, such as Autoexec.bat and Himem.sys
- Operating System files, such as Explore.exe and Gdi.exe
- Application software, such as Winword.exe
- Data files, such as Patients.dbf

The Operating System itself is a frequent target of virus infection, leaving you unable to start Windows on a compromised computer. At a more basic level, the Boot Sector of the hard drive is sometimes deleted or made inoperative by a virus. Such an infection would prevent you from booting the computer at all.

## Corrupting the Computer's BIOS

A less common, but very destructive, type of virus is the CIH family of viruses. These viruses corrupt the BIOS, which is a vital part of your computer's main system board. This type of damage leaves you unable to boot the computer, even from a floppy Boot Disk. It is rare for one of these viruses to accomplish its objective, but when it does, the damage is difficult to repair.

## Other Forms of Damage

Most of the remaining forms of virus damage happen within the normal operation of the Windows Operating System. Here are two common examples:

- Filling up the computer's hard drive, by copying files repetitively
- Opening multiple programs, until all free System Resources have been exhausted

### Interfering With Anti-Virus Software

Generally since 2002, virus behavior has included programming that is designed to keep the virus from being detected or removed by the popular AV programs. Some common symptoms of this behavior include the following:

- Deleting or disabling any AV programs found on the infected computer
- Preventing installation or execution of AV programs
- Preventing execution of virus repair programs
- Preventing access to Web sites of AV software vendors

### Turning Infected Computers Into Zombies

Another increasingly common payload of the newer viruses is to commandeer the infected computer and have that machine carry out the wishes of the virus writer. Thus far, this technique has been used in two different ways, both of which can be very disruptive.

## Launching DoS or DDoS Attacks

One approach used by some viruses is to cause a Denial of Service (DoS) attack on a server or group of servers. A DoS is designed to send a high volume of message traffic to the targeted server in a very short period of time. The objective of such an attack is to overload the server to the extent that it can no longer handle its normal traffic.

When a virus is widespread, it can coordinate the sending of thousands, even millions, of messages to the targeted server through its network of hijacked, "zombie" computers. Such a large-scale assault is known as a Distributed Denial of Service, or DDoS attack. With a large enough DDoS attempt, it would be possible to affect the responsiveness and availability of the entire Internet.

When you hear of an organization's Web site, such as that of an airline reservation system or an ATM network, being shut down, that is the intended result of a DDoS attack. Perhaps the most successful example of such an attack was the massive disruption wrought by the Slammer (also known as Sapphire) worm.

Other DDoS attacks have targeted various government and military agencies. Some other recent targets of these campaigns have been anti-spam Web sites, including www.spamhaus.com, www.spamcop.net, and www.spews.org.

A more recent development in the use of Zombie computers is to use the threat of a DDoS as a form of extortion. If the targeted organization doesn't pay the price demanded by the person who controls the Zombie network, they may find their servers crashed.

## Using Zombie Computers as Spam Relays

Another increasingly common use of infected computers is to turn these computers into e-mail servers, relaying spam messages on behalf of spammers. Two effective examples of this technique thus far are the Sobig.F and Netsky. P worms. These have been two of the most widespread computer viruses in history as of this writing.

In most cases of Zombie computers, the owners and operators of the computers involved are not even aware they are participating. This background operation improves the likelihood the attempt will be successful.

## No Apparent Symptoms

One more result of a virus infection of which you need to be aware is "No apparent symptoms." Many modern viruses don't reveal themselves in any way that would be apparent to the typical computer user, so it's essential that you scan your computer for virus infection on a regular basis.

# Chapter 8
## How Viruses Are Spread

Since the introduction of the first computer virus, the methods used to distribute new viruses have evolved through several generations. A look at the time line of virus replication can lead to a better understanding of techniques that are common in spreading today's viruses to a worldwide audience of unsuspecting computer users.

## How The Original Viruses Spread

When viruses first began spreading from one computer to another, there was only one transport mechanism available to accomplish this replication. That method was to place the virus on a floppy disk in the infected computer. When that diskette was inserted into another computer, the virus infected its new host.

While floppy disks are used infrequently these days, they do still represent one of the methods that can be used by any virus to distribute the malicious code. The same can be said of any removable media in use on modern computers, including Zip disks, recordable CD and DVD media, etc.

Another method used by early viruses, although with a more modest success rate, was by way of files downloaded through Bulletin Board Systems, or BBSs. These on-line time-sharing services, usually through slow, dial-up modems, were the prehistoric ancestors of today's Internet communications.

Most computer users of that generation were not on-line at all, and BBS systems were notoriously user-unfriendly. Virtually all computers at the time were text-based, running DOS applications; the Graphical User Interface of Windows had not yet become popular. Consequently, virus distribution via BBS was a fairly rare occurrence.

# The Second Generation of Viruses

The second generation of virus distribution became possible as more computers were connected over Local Area Networks, or LANs. For the virus writers, it was a fairly simple task to send their infected files from one computer to another across the LAN.

As LANs evolved into Wide Area Networks, and the Internet was formed, the virus problem has grown exponentially. The more computers are connected, the more paths are available for viruses to spread and wreak their damage on unprepared computer users.

# The Current Generation

In one form or another, the Internet is used to spread most viruses and other forms of malware today. In some cases, links on Web sites may lead to virus infection; such links are the most common source of spyware being installed on vulnerable computers.

Chat sessions and newsgroups are high-risk sources of virus infection. Users of chat programs such as IRC and ICQ should exercise extreme caution in this environment. An open-source program named Jabber has also been identified as vulnerable in this arena.

## The Exposure of Instant Messaging

As Instant Messaging systems have increased in popularity, they have also become more tempting targets for malware. Most of these systems offer little protection against viruses and other malicious software. In some cases, protection is available in these programs but is disabled by default.

If you are using any of these Instant Messaging programs, it is highly recommended that you refer to the program documentation to learn more about its vulnerabilities and the steps you can take to protect your system from infection:

- AOL Instant Messenger
- Microsoft Messenger
- MSN Messenger
- Yahoo! Messenger

While it is possible to receive a virus through any of the means listed above, the most common distribution method for virus transmission in the current computing environment is through e-mail messages.

## Transmission of Viruses Via E-Mail

Regardless of the e-mail program you are using, there are viruses that can be carried through the e-mail messages you receive. In the early days of viruses that were spread through e-mail messages, the virus was contained in an attachment; when the attachment was opened, the virus infected that computer.

As virus writers became more sophisticated, they learned how to create virus code that executed as soon as the infected message was read. Of course, the virus had no way of knowing when the message was actually read; in fact, the malware was executed as soon as the message was opened in the e-mail program.

## Preview Pane – The Weakest Link In Your E-Mail Program

This technique also carried an unfortunate side effect. By default, most e-mail programs automatically open the current message as a convenience to the user. The message then appears, usually in the lower right-hand section of the e-mail program known as the Preview Pane.

Since the message must be opened in order to appear in the Preview Pane, this behavior allows viruses to spread without the message even having been read by the unsuspecting e-mail recipient. This vulnerability is the major downside of the Preview Pane.

It should be noted that the early viruses that used this technique were taking advantage of a known flaw in Microsoft's Outlook Express program. Microsoft has long since fixed that particular vulnerability by means of a Windows Critical Update, so this technique no longer serves the purpose exploited by these viruses.

Even so, the Preview Pane still presents an unacceptable exposure to other approaches used by some virus writers. By default, any e-mail message that contains HTML code will be executed when opened in the Preview Pane. HTML code is the set of programming instructions that allow e-mail messages to include graphics, photographs, fancy fonts, colors, and other elements that improve the visual appeal of the message. Those who would harm your computer could use such code for a wide range of malicious purposes.

## Your Choice of E-Mail Programs

To a certain extent, your vulnerability to e-mail borne viruses depends upon the e-mail program you use. Since most virus writers want to infect as many computers as possible with any given virus, and Outlook Express is the most widely used e-mail program, it is the most frequent target of malware.

Second on the popularity list, especially among malware writers who want to disrupt businesses, is Microsoft Outlook. The fact that Microsoft markets Outlook as their business e-mail program, combined with the high degree of anti-Microsoft sentiment among virus writers and hackers, makes it a tempting target.

But regardless of the e-mail program you use, you may be susceptible to viruses and other forms of malware that are distributed via e-mail messages. Even users of AOL, CompuServe, Eudora, MSN, Netscape, or other lesser-known e-mail programs are all at some risk.

## Where and How Viruses Find New E-Mail Addresses to Infect

Once a virus has infected a computer by way of e-mail transmission, its first mission is to spread itself to other computers through infected e-mail messages. Modern viruses will attempt to find e-mail addresses in two places: the Address Book used by that computer, and previous e-mail messages and other documents stored on the computer.

Those other documents that are examined typically include those that have been produced by word processing, spreadsheet, and database programs. Virus writers know that many users store lists of e-mail addresses in such files.

As an example of how much damage may be caused by this approach, consider an e-mail message you may have received and saved on your computer, that was sent to your e-mail address and multiple additional addresses. If those addresses were placed in the To: field of the message, or the Cc: field, they are now stored on your computer.

In this scenario, any virus that uses this technique to replicate itself can find these additional addresses and attempt to infect them. Note that the addresses do not need to be in your address book in order to be susceptible to this type of attack.

## Vulnerabilities in Your Internet Browser

A common entry point for viruses and other malware is the Browser you use to access the Internet. As the most widely used browser, Microsoft's Internet Explorer has been exploited frequently by those who would infect vulnerable computers. Many of those attacks have taken advantage of known flaws in Internet Explorer.

In almost every case of such an exploit, Microsoft has produced and distributed a Critical Update that removes the vulnerability. By keeping your Windows Updates current, you minimize the chance that a virus can successfully penetrate the defenses of Windows or Internet Explorer.

Even so, an increasing number of concerned Internet users have begun switching to an alternative browser, other than Internet Explorer. Their reasoning is that other browsers are not susceptible to the same type of exploits and thus are a safer choice of browser software.

If you decide to use a different browser, there are quite a few choices available. Some Internet Service Providers include their own browser software, such as AOL, Time-Warner, and Yahoo! Netscape Navigator has its long-term users and advocates, as does Opera. The most popular alternative in recent months is Mozilla's FireFox Browser.

But is an alternative browser really any more secure than Internet Explorer? In case you have been led to believe that these other programs are immune to viruses and other malware, you've been sadly misled. Every week new flaws are found in these alternative programs, just as they are in Internet Explorer. In many cases the new vulnerabilities are different between browsers, but the point is that no browser will ever offer complete safety from malware.

To a certain extent, the main reason Internet Explorer is the most frequent target of malware is its market dominance. The virus producers want to devote their effort to the program that represents the largest audience of their intended victims; as long as that's Internet Explorer, most viruses will target it. When FireFox gains a large enough market share, it will become the new target of choice.

Regardless of which browser you use, you can maximize its security in two important ways. First, be sure you apply any Critical Updates that are developed to fix security flaws. Then, spend some time learning about the security settings included in your browser. You'll probably find some default values that leave your computer unnecessarily exposed to some types of malware attack. This subject is discussed in further detail in Chapter 13, "Preventive Measures."

## A New Twist On Virus Distribution

Another method of spreading viruses was first used very successfully by the Blaster worm (MSBlast.exe), in August, 2003. This virus did not spread via e-mail, infected links on Web sites, or any of the other traditional distribution methods. Instead, it randomly generated TCP/IP addresses and attempted to infect any computer that had a matching address.

Like so many virus attacks, Blaster was able to cause such widespread damage by exploiting a known vulnerability in the Microsoft Windows 2000 and Windows XP Operating Systems. Microsoft had issued a Critical Update to correct this problem weeks before Blaster was released in the wild.

Any computers that had installed this Critical Update were not affected by Blaster. Nor were computers that connected to the Internet through a firewall, since a firewall insulates the computer's address from the outside world of the Internet. But for those users whose computers were connected directly to the Internet, and who had not applied the Critical Update, there was a high likelihood that Blaster would cause severe problems.

## What Computers Are Susceptible To Viruses?

We'll wrap up this chapter with two important points about the spread of viruses. First, there is no such thing as an Operating System that is immune to viruses. Although the great majority of viruses target the Microsoft Windows Operating Systems, virtually every platform has been the victim of some virus infections. This certainly includes Macintosh, Unix, Linux, and IBM Mainframe and AS/400 environments.

Finally, it's important to understand that many recent viruses don't reveal their presence with obvious symptoms in the early stages of infection. The longer a virus remains on a computer undetected, the more damage it will cause. So, when dealing with the possibility of virus infection, always remember that time is the enemy.

# Chapter 9
## Dealing With Spam

There is universal agreement these days that unsolicited commercial e-mail (UCE), better known as spam, is the most significant obstacle to a productive e-mail experience. Some pundits have even gone so far as to suggest that the proliferation of spam will destroy the viability of e-mail as a means of business communications.

While that may be somewhat of an overstatement, it is clear that spam is a major source of irritation and frustration among those who use e-mail on a regular basis. According to some of the latest statistics, spam accounts for well over 50 percent of all e-mail traffic destined for the average computer user. The more you can do to reduce this clutter in your inbox, the more enjoyable and productive your computing experience will be.

In the belief that the spam problem could be eliminated, or at least substantially controlled, by legislation, in 2003 the U. S. Congress passed a new law with this objective. Titled The CAN-SPAM Act of 2003 (Controlling the Assault of Non-Solicited Pornography and Marketing Act), this law became effective January 1, 2004.

Without going into all the reasons, suffice it to say that this law has had very little effect in reducing the spread of unsolicited commercial e-mail. The law does provide for civil penalties and may serve as a starting point for reform, but most e-mail users would be hard pressed to find that the new law has reduced the volume of spam they receive.

## The Original Kind of Spam

For the sake of clarification, we are not talking about Spam, the delicious luncheon meat produced by Hormel Foods Corporation in Austin, Minnesota. Hormel introduced its product in 1937, and by 1959 the company had already produced over one billion cans of Spam Luncheon Meat.

The company does have a sense of humor, though, as well as a sense of history. Any time you're in the area, be sure to stop in and visit Hormel's Spam Museum in Austin, Minnesota. Opened in 2001, this 16,500-square-foot museum is open 360 days per year, and there is no admission fee. Call 1-800-LUV-SPAM for directions and further details.

It's unfortunate that the name of their product has been applied to this modern-day menace. This association is commonly related to a Monty Python skit, although the direct relationship between the skit and junk e-mail is a bit unclear. Here is a link to one (of many) site where you may see and hear the original skit:  http://www.detritus. org/spam/skit.html

## Similarity of Spam and Viruses

As a fringe benefit, when you learn how to reduce the spam on your system, you will also greatly reduce your exposure to viruses and other forms of malware. Since the distribution method is similar among all these attackers, spam prevention = virus prevention = malware prevention.

The first objective of spammers (those who send out this junk) is to convince you to open their message and read it. They frequently try to accomplish this by using misleading or false information, in the From: field or the Subject: of the message.

Remember, you may cause your computer to become infected just by opening a virus-infected e-mail message. And by opening certain spam messages, you may expose yourself or your coworkers or children to graphic images and/or language that you would find offensive. So, your first objective is to not open any e-mail message that contains spam or a virus.

Fortunately, there are many clues you can use to identify suspicious e-mail messages and delete them without opening them. In order to be as fully protected as possible, it is essential that you turn off the Preview Pane in your e-mail program, as described in Chapter 13.

Each column of an e-mail message may contain clues that it is spam or a virus, and should be deleted instead of being opened and read. Here are some signs to look out for.

## Priority

First, the Priority column is frequently used by spammers to make their message appear to be urgent, and thus encourage you to open it immediately. Any time you see an e-mail message with High Priority (indicated by a red exclamation mark), unless you know the sender, the message is almost certainly spam.

On the other hand, some spammers are now marking their messages Low Priority (indicated by a blue down-arrow), in the belief that this will increase your likelihood of opening them. Don't fall for that one, either!

## Attachment

The next column that should raise your suspicion is the Attachment indicator (a black paper clip) associated with this message. If an attachment is consistent with the sender and the subject of the e-mail, you can probably assume it's legitimate. But if there's any doubt in your mind, check it out before opening the attachment.

While attachments are no longer necessary for viruses to proliferate, they are still the most common method of spreading a virus from one infected computer to another. Attachments may also be used by hackers or unscrupulous advertisers to install software on your computer that will monitor your computing and Internet activity. That information may then be used for nefarious purposes, without your knowledge or consent.

In many cases of malware that is spread through an e-mail attachment, there is a very obvious clue that lets the careful e-mail user know not to open the attachment. If the file name of the attachment contains more than one suffix, you can be fairly certain it is a virus or other unwelcome programming.

An example of such a file name would be Your Refund.doc.pif. While the file name and its initial suffix may appear legitimate, the presence of the second suffix (or file type) is a sure indication that this file is not what it purports to be.

## From

The next column of concern is the From: field. You will find that most spammers do not show their actual identity here. They may show a fictitious name that sounds legitimate, or a company name that is not the true source of the e-mail message (Microsoft, Norton, and the major ISPs are very popular targets here).

Or, this field may contain what appears to be an actual e-mail address, although those addresses are usually falsified as well. The point is, you can't trust the name or e-mail address that appears in the From: field. It's just too easy for the spammers and virus writers to "spoof" that address and make it appear safe to you.

## Subject

The Subject: of the e-mail message may identify this message as spam or other malware in a number of ways. Here are some common examples of subject lines used by spammers:

- Blank or empty Subject
- "Hi," "Hello," "Greetings," or similar salutations
- Your name inserted in the Subject, especially if it is all in capital letters
- Your e-mail name (the part of your e-mail address preceding the @) appears here
- A blank space or the word "null" where your name should have been inserted
- Random group of extra characters and/or numbers included after the Subject

Of course, there are a number of words the Subject might contain, that would give you a pretty good indication the message is spam. Here are some all-too-common examples:

- Cards, Pay, Satellite, Toy
- Cartridge, Ink, Toner
- Credit, Interest, Million, Money, Mortgage, Rate
- Drugs, Medication, Pharmacy, Prescription
- Enlarge, Viagra, Weight
- ADV (Only the reputable spammers will use this!)

In addition to these overused words, various terms describing body parts and sexual acts are frequently included in the Subject field. Obviously, these messages didn't come from a friend or customer, and they should be considered risky to open.

In most cases, you will be able to easily identify spam and other suspicious messages by looking for these obvious clues. But for those messages that you don't recognize as coming from a trusted correspondent, yet do not want to delete arbitrarily, it's time to move on to Level 2 procedures for malware detection.

## An Initial Look At Message Headers

The next step in validating an incoming e-mail message involves examining the headers of the message for further clues. Chapter 12 of this book includes a more detailed discussion of the e-mail headers and their full meaning, but the next few paragraphs will describe the common characteristics of spam and other malware that you can find here.

The method you will use to examine the headers of an e-mail message will vary depending upon the e-mail program you are using. The examples on the following pages are from Microsoft's Outlook Express program; you will find screens similar to these in other e-mail programs.

To view these headers in Outlook Express, right-click on the suspicious message, and choose Properties. There are two tabs within this dialog box, which contain all of the information you are likely to need in order to determine whether you should delete the message.

On the General tab, you will find the Subject: and the From: address of the sender. The format of the From: address is "User Name" <e-mail address>, which is intended to let you see the actual e-mail address of the sender. In the case of spam or other malware, you will frequently find that these two components don't match.

For example, a legitimate e-mail message would contain a User Name such as John Smith, and an e-mail address similar to jsmith@bigcompany.com. On the other hand, a malware message may contain a User Name such as Susie Hotchick and an e-mail address something like sqzlijjm@pornsource.com.

Such a mismatch would be a virtual guarantee that you should delete the message. Another common tip-off would be the absence of a User Name – in other words, just the supposed e-mail address of the sender appears, enclosed in brackets.

## "Spoofing" the "From" Address

The term "supposed e-mail address" is used here as a reminder that you cannot necessarily trust the address contained in the e-mail header. This field is relatively easy for spammers and hackers to falsify, so you should use it only as a starting point to determine the true identity of the sender.

You may be surprised to find your own e-mail address between the brackets on this tab. An increasing number of spam messages are being sent out with the recipient's e-mail address shown as the sender's address as well. Unless you know the message in question came from your computer, this is another obvious example of spam or a virus.

## Country Codes

The other valuable information you can derive from the e-mail address shown here is to look for messages sent from foreign domains. Every country with access to the Internet has been assigned a two-letter alphabetic code, which will appear as the final portion of that domain name. For example, jsmith@bigcompany.co.uk. You will also notice that foreign domains typically use .co.xx as the suffix, instead of the .com that is most commonly used in United States domains.

Domains registered to U. S. organizations may use the .us country code, but this is usually omitted for the sake of simplicity. A complete listing of Country

Codes is contained in Appendix A of this book. Unless you are expecting e-mail from someone in a country other than the United States, you can safely delete any messages from foreign domains.

The next level of sleuthing through the e-mail headers involves additional information found on the Details tab of the Properties for this message. This screen is rich with clues that may prove an incoming e-mail message is up to no good.

## To: and Cc:

One of the most obvious clues on this screen is the content of the To: field. You may be surprised to see that it contains an e-mail address other than yours. If that's the case, there's a good possibility this message is malware. This may be normal behavior, though, for messages you receive from a listserv or a legitimate e-mail subscription.

If your e-mail address doesn't appear in the To: field, you may see it in the Cc: line. If it's not there either, then the message was sent with your address in the Bcc: field. This is the preferred method of sending an e-mail message to multiple recipients.

If you see multiple addressees in the To: or Cc: fields, that is another indication that the message in question is some form of malware. Delete the message immediately, unless you recognize the sender as someone you know, who doesn't know the proper way to send such a message.

## Other Headers

Another indication of the sender misrepresenting him/herself can be found by looking for a Reply-To: header on this tab of Properties. If the address shown there doesn't match the address in the From: field, that's another red flag for you.

There are three more headers you may find on this tab that will tip you off to a message you don't want to open. These header fields are sometimes inserted by your Internet Service Provider, or by one of the "relay stations" that handled the message between the time it left the sender's computer and the time it arrived on yours.

You may see a header line that reads "X-Header-Overseas: Mail.from.Overseas.source," followed by an IP address. Here again, unless you are expecting mail from foreign domains, this is another indication of a message that you would best be advised not to open.

Another header that raises serious suspicion is one that reads "X-Header-NoReverseIP: IP.name.lookup.failed," again followed by an IP address. This message indicates that the alleged sender's domain name does not match the IP address from which it was sent. This mismatch is a clear indication that the sender is making a serious effort to keep you from knowing the actual source of the message. Off to the Deleted Items Folder with this one!

## Bogus IP Addresses

If any of these IP addresses begin with 192.168 as the first two numbers, this is a subtle indication of a falsified address. This address is commonly used by computers on a Local Area Network, but it is never used by computers connected directly to the Internet.

There are three additional IP addresses that will never be routed across the Internet. If the first number in the IP address is 10, or if the first two numbers are 169.254 or 172.16, the address has been forged.

Finally, you may see a header that says "X-MailScanner: Found to be clean," which sounds reassuring. But be advised, the only time this header appears is in e-mail messages that actually do contain a virus. So much for truth in labeling!

The following pages provide examples of messages that contain some of the suspicious elements that lead us to suspect that they are spam. By using a few simple steps to find out more details of these messages, we can validate or rebut those suspicions. Figure 9.1 illustrates some actual e-mail messages received, as viewed in Microsoft Outlook Express.

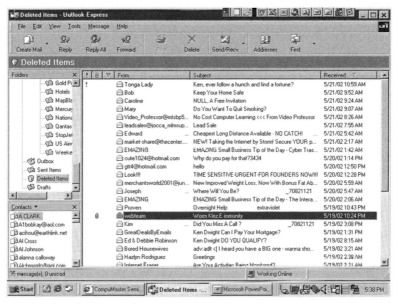

*Figure 9.1 A collection of e-mail messages with suspicious characteristics.*

## Suspicious Signs in Subject Lines

Even a brief glance at the messages on this screen reveals numerous examples of the clues discussed earlier in this chapter. For example, the first entry, from "Tonga Lady," is marked high priority (!), and has the name "Ken" inserted in the subject line.

The third entry, from "Caroline," tried to insert the recipient's name in the Subject field but failed, as a result of a programming error. Thus, NULL appears and provides a clear tip-off that this is a spam message.

Two of these messages use suspicious one-word Subjects – "hello" and "Greetings" – and three more have random numbers at the end of the Subject line. One entry, from "Bored Housewives," is considerate enough to identify itself as an advertising message, and even goes so far as to let the recipient know that it includes adult content.

Now let's look at two of these messages in greater detail. Looking first at the message above the highlighted line, there are three elements that would indicate this is likely to be spam. First, we see that it appears to come from "Proven," who is not a sender we recognize; the Subject, "Overnight Help," has no particular meaning to us, and is followed by the word "extraviolet," which is offset by multiple blank spaces.

By right-clicking on this message and choosing Properties, we see the screen in Figure 9.2.

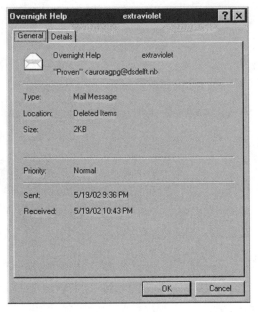

*Figure 9.2*
*The General tab helps*
*confirm our suspicions.*

On the General tab, the name in the From: field is further identified by the e-mail address of the sender, enclosed in brackets. In this case, the sender is shown as auroragpg@dsdelft.nl. The two-letter Country Code at the end of this address identifies this sender as being from The Netherlands. Unless you were expecting an e-mail from someone in The Netherlands, you can pretty safely assume this is a spam message.

It is important to note here that this address is easy to forge, or "spoof", so you can't always depend on the accuracy of what is shown at this stage. Most spammers won't take the time or effort to modify the From: address, though, so this field usually reflects the actual address of the sender.

In case you're still not sure, you can click on the Details tab and see the header information. This subject is covered in greater detail in Chapter 12, but this chapter presents the basic information you will need to make a spam/no-spam determination. The Details tab for this message is shown in Figure 9.3.

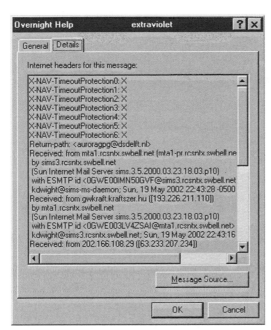

*Figure 9.3*
*The Details tab*
*reveals the e-mail*
*headers for this*
*message.*

Although all the servers through which this message passed are not visible on this screen, scrolling through the list revealed that the message had traveled through Hungary, Poland, and the Netherlands on its way to this computer. Notice that the server that handled the message last was in Hungary (gwkraft. kraftszer.hu), and scrolling down in this screen reveals a previous server in Poland (.pl).

Sometimes the message headers shown in this view will include a line "X-Header-Overseas: Mail.from.Overseas.source," which is another indication that the message originated outside of a United States domain. For a complete listing of the 254 two-letter Country Codes, see Appendix A of this book.

Based on what we've found in these headers, this message is clearly spam and can be deleted safely.

Next, let's examine the message at the bottom of the screen, which appears to come from Hazlyn Rodriguez, with a Subject of "Greetings." At a glance, there are at least two reasons to suspect this message is spam: Hazlyn Rodriguez is not a name we recognize, and "Greetings" is one of those suspicious Subjects.

When we right-click on this message and choose Properties, we see the screen in Figure 9.4.

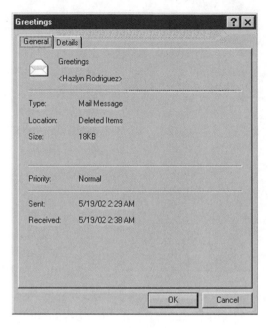

*Figure 9.4*
*This message does*
*not contain a valid*
*e-mail address for*
*the sender.*

Now we have one more reason to be suspicious of this message. Notice that there is no valid e-mail address shown for the sender. The name Hazlyn Rodriguez is shown in brackets; normally the displayed name will be shown first, followed by the sender's e-mail address enclosed in brackets.

Going to the Details tab, we see the beginning of the e-mail headers shown in Figure 9.5.

*Figure 9.5*
*The headers in this*
*message start off*
*looking fairly*
*normal.*

Nothing in this screen appears conclusive, as far as helping to determine whether or not this message is spam. So, it's necessary to scroll down further in this dialog box, to the continuation of its headers as shown in Figure 9.6.

*Figure 9.6*
*The continuation of*
*the e-mail headers*
*proves that this*
*message is spam.*

Now, our suspicions are confirmed. Look at all those e-mail addresses in the Cc: field of this message, in alphabetical order! It's unlikely this is a message worthy of remaining on the computer.

In addition to this message being spam, it also violates one of the most basic rules of netiquette; by listing all of the addresses in the Cc: field, every recipient will have access to all those e-mail addresses. They, in turn, are exposed to additional spam and viruses, as we will discuss in Chapter 13.

## Reducing your spam input

Now that you have a more thorough idea of the various ways spam messages may identify themselves, you are better prepared to reduce the flow of these annoying messages into your Inbox. There are a number of methods available to you that will help in this effort.

## To Remove, or not to remove

In most cases, one method to avoid using is the "Remove me" link found in most spam e-mail messages. Following this link will frequently increase your spam input, instead of reducing it. This happens because most spammers have no interest in removing your name and e-mail address from their list.

When you click on the "Remove me" link, you have just verified to the sender that this e-mail address is valid, and that you received and read their message. This qualification process makes your e-mail address that much more valuable to spammers, giving them an extra incentive to resell your address to others who will add it to their distribution list.

You can safely use this process when dealing with well-known, reputable public companies. These businesses are more concerned about their image and customer satisfaction than the short-term revenue they could generate by selling your e-mail address. But if the sender is not a household name, just delete the message without replying to it.

You would be well advised to be particularly leery of plain-text messages. If the sender is not sufficiently computer savvy to make their message visually appealing, they are also unlikely to have a legitimate removal process.

## Spam Filtering in your e-mail program

All the popular e-mail programs provide some tools that you can use to greatly reduce the number of spam messages you need to examine manually. In using these tools, though, you need to realize that no automated process for spam identification is perfect.

No matter how well crafted your spam criteria may be, some actual spam messages will escape detection and make their way into your Inbox. On the other hand, an occasional legitimate message will fit some aspects of the spam definitions and be handled accordingly, causing you to miss it.

The most widely used tools for spam prevention in most e-mail programs are the Blocked Sender List and Message Rules. Any time you receive an e-mail message that you identify as spam, you have the option to add that sender to your Blocked Sender List.

Unfortunately, that approach rarely serves its intended purpose any longer. Most of the serious spammers today use a simple technique that keeps their future messages from being blocked by a Blocked Sender List.

If you look at the e-mail address in the From: field of most spam messages, you'll find that it consists of a random set of characters preceding the @ in the address. So, if you add jjklixqz@spammer.com to your Blocked Sender List and the next message from that same spammer uses an address of lxqziimp@spammer.com, it breezes right past this filter.

## Mail Rules in your E-Mail Program

As a practical matter, the Blocked Sender List has pretty much outlived its usefulness. You can accomplish the intended result, albeit with more effort, by using Mail Rules instead. The next few pages include examples of some Mail Rules you will probably want to add to your e-mail program.

These examples are based on Microsoft Outlook Express, but most modern e-mail programs offer similar capabilities. These same concepts apply across all e-mail programs.

The first Rule you may want to define is one that will identify messages that did not contain your e-mail address in the To: field of the message. Here are the steps for defining such a rule. After choosing Tools from the Menu Bar, then selecting Message Rules and Mail, you will see a screen similar to the one shown in Figure 9.7.

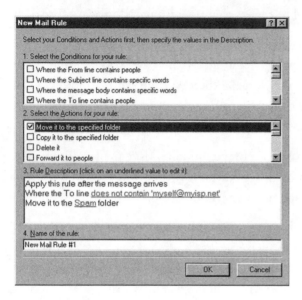

*Figure 9.7 This screen is used to define a Mail Rule in Outlook Express, sending to the Spam folder any message that did not include your e-mail address in the To line.*

This example of specifying a Mail Rule in Outlook Express illustrates the option to filter messages based on the contents of the To line, as specified in Box 1 If the given condition is met, the Action specified in Box 2 is to move that message to the specified folder.

Box 3 shows the parameters that have been defined for that filter and allows you to edit those parameters. In this case, if the To line does not contain the address myself@myisp.net, the message will be moved to the Spam folder.

Here are the exact steps you'll need to follow in order to create this Rule on your computer, using your e-mail address and your choice of folders to contain the selected messages.

First, in the New Mail Rule dialog box, place check marks in the following boxes: In Box 1, check "Where the To line contains people," and in Box 2, check "Move it to the specified folder," as shown in Figure 9.8.

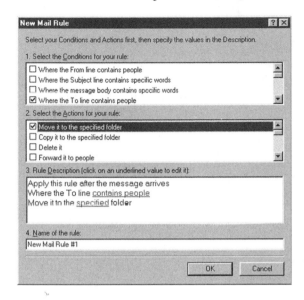

*Figure 9.8 These are the first two steps in defining this Mail Rule.*

Next, go to Box 3 and click on the hyperlink "contains people." That opens the dialog box shown in Figure 9.9.

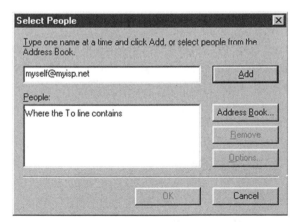

*Figure 9.9 This dialog box lets you specify the e-mail addresses to be included or excluded in this Mail Rule.*

Enter your e-mail address in the first line, and click Add. Then click Options...,
which opens the dialog box shown in Figure 9.10.

*Figure 9.10 This dialog box lets
you specify that the Rule applies
if the message does not contain
the indicated e-mail address.*

Choose the second option in Item 1, to catch messages that do not contain
your e-mail address in the To: line. Click OK here, then OK again on the Select
People dialog box, and this part of the rule definition is complete.

Finally, go back to Box 3 of the New Mail Rule and click on the hyperlink
"specified," where you choose the folder to contain messages identified by
this rule. You may want to create a folder named Spam to hold these messages, or send them directly to the Deleted Items folder if you wish.

This simple filter can be used to segregate multiple-recipient messages from
those which are sent only to your e-mail address. This will reduce the amount
of spam in your Inbox, but may also have an unintended consequence. Any
message that is sent to multiple recipients, listed in the "Cc:" or "Bcc:" fields,
will be intercepted by this rule.

This approach may treat as spam e-zines or other subscription-based e-mails,
as well as messages from individuals who have included your e-mail address
on a distribution list. For this reason, it is suggested that you not use this rule
to automatically delete messages that meet this criterion.

## Filtering on the Subject Line

There are two more filters you may want to define, that will identify a high percentage of spam messages. First, you may define a Mail Rule that looks for specific words in the Subject line of the message. As a starting point, we'll define a rule that contains some of the words listed earlier in this chapter. Figure 9.11 illustrates the starting point for this Rule.

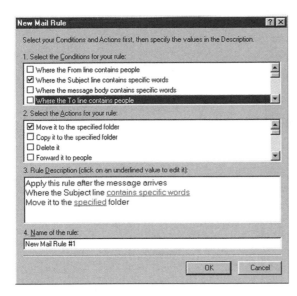

*Figure 9.11 This dialog box lets you define a Mail Rule that filters incoming messages based on words found in the Subject of the message.*

Once you've checked the appropriate boxes in sections 1 and 2, click on the hyperlink to "contains specific words," and you'll be taken to the dialog box shown in Figure 9.12.

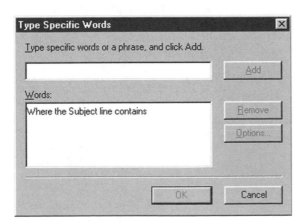

*Figure 9.12 This dialog box lets you list the specific words to be included in this Mail Rule.*

In the first line of this dialog box, enter a word or phrase, then click Add. You may add as many search terms here as you like, but to keep the list manageable it should probably contain no more than about 15 terms. An example of this Rule when complete is shown in Figure 9.13.

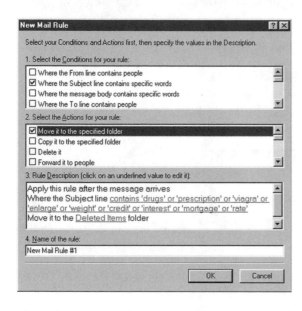

*Figure 9.13 This Mail Rule will cause any incoming message to be moved to the Deleted Items Folder if its Subject contains any of the words listed in the Rule Description.*

If you have more than 15 words or phrases that you want to use as filters in this manner, you may define multiple rules to accommodate that need. In fact, Outlook Express includes the option to copy an existing rule, which you can then modify to include the additional terms desired.

The potential problem with this type of Mail Rule is the literal nature of the words or terms that are defined in these rules. Many spammers, especially the more unscrupulous ones, deliberately misspell the words you are likely to have included in such rules, to avoid detection of their messages.

For example, instead of "Viagra," the Subject line may contain "v1agra," or "v-i-a-g-r-a," or some other obvious misspelling that a human would recognize but an automated rule would not. This is just another example of the techniques used by spammers to defeat any attempt at blocking their messages.

## Filtering on Sender's E-Mail Address

Another Mail Rule that can shield you from a lot of spam is, in effect, your customized version of a Blocked Sender List. You can achieve this capability by defining a Rule that examines the sender's e-mail address. The first two steps to define such a Rule are shown in Figure 9.14.

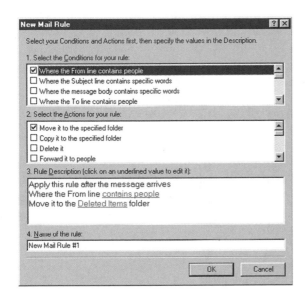

*Figure 9.14 This dialog box lets you specify that certain senders are to be included in this Mail Rule, and their messages moved to the Deleted Items folder when found.*

With the boxes in sections 1 and 2 checked as shown in Figure 9.14, click on the hyperlink to "contains people," and you'll see the dialog box shown in Figure 9.15.

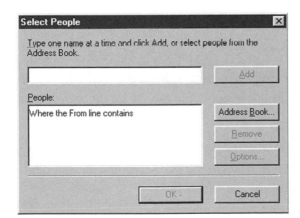

*Figure 9.15 This dialog box lets you specify the e-mail address or addresses to be included in this Mail Rule.*

Here, you will enter only the domain names of the spammers you want to block. By using this technique instead of the Blocked Sender List, whatever prefix the spammer uses before the @, any message from that domain is caught by this Rule. An example of the finished Rule appears in Figure 9.16.

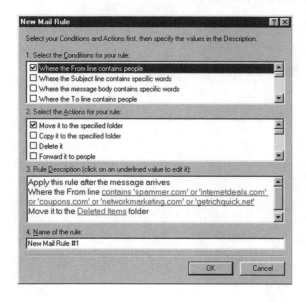

*Figure 9.16 This Mail Rule causes messages received from any of the specified domains to be moved directly into the Deleted Items folder.*

In the same way as the Subject Line Rule, you will probably need to define multiple From Line Rules to include the ever-increasing number of spammers you wish to block. To stay ahead of the offenders, it will be necessary to update these rules continuously.

## Filtering in Microsoft Outlook

Your e-mail program may permit more extensive filtering than the choices provided by Outlook Express. For example, Microsoft Outlook 2000 provides additional options that can help you eliminate many more incoming spam messages.

In order to define Mail Rules in Outlook 2000, you will click on Tools in the Menu Bar, then select Rules Wizard. Click on New..., and you will see a screen similar to the one shown in Figure 9.17.

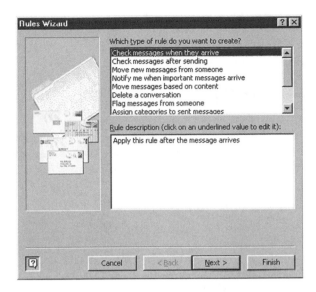

*Figure 9.17 The Rules Wizard in Microsoft Outlook offers numerous types of Rules that you can define.*

Most of the filtering of incoming messages will be done in the "Check messages when they arrive" category. Select this option, then click Next, and a screen similar to the one shown in Figure 9.18 will appear.

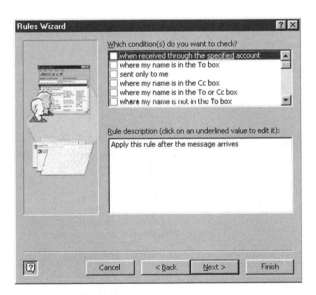

*Figure 9.18 The Rules Wizard lets you specify the selection criteria.*

You'll notice that the first conditions shown in the list are similar to those in Outlook Express, and the way they are used is virtually identical to the steps covered earlier in this chapter. But as you scroll further down the list, you come to a group of filters that allow you to check for specific words. That section of the filters is illustrated in Figure 9.19.

*Figure 9.19*
*The Rules Wizard*
*in Microsoft Outlook*
*provides a wider range*
*of filtering options than*
*those offered by*
*Outlook Express.*

By checking the box for "specific words in the message header," you can filter out messages with the undesirable headers discussed earlier in this chapter. For example, Figure 9.20 illustrates one rule that most users in the United States would want to include.

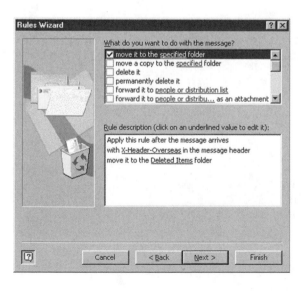

*Figure 9.20*
*This Rule causes*
*any messages received*
*from overseas domains*
*to be moved directly*
*into the Deleted*
*Items folder.*

Another useful enhancement offered by Outlook 2000 is the ability to allow for exceptions to the rule. Figure 9.21 illustrates a partial listing of the exceptions you can define.

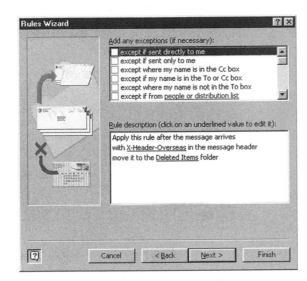

*Figure 9.21*
*The Rules Wizard*
*in Microsoft Outlook*
*allows for exceptions*
*to the Rules*
*you have defined.*

As you can see, Outlook 2000 gives you a lot more choices in filtering incoming e-mail than those included in Outlook Express. For many e-mail users, this capability alone justifies the upgrade to Outlook, which is a component of the Microsoft Office suite.

If setting up Mail Rules sounds like a lot of work, it definitely can be fairly time-consuming. There is another approach that can take most of this effort out of your hands: Choose an Internet Service Provider who provides spam filtering as a standard (or optional) service for their customers.

An increasing number of ISPs are offering such a service to their subscribers, with varying degrees of success. Some of these spam filters are very effective; many are less so. With the current level of spam activity, a good ISP will block at least 75 percent of the messages from arriving in your Inbox.

With or without filtering by your ISP, you may prefer to use a third-party utility program for this purpose; there are many from which to choose. Here are some current products that have received positive reviews in various trade journals:

- · iHateSpam (from Sunbelt Software, www.sunbeltsoftware.com)
- · Norton AntiSpam (from Symantec, www.symantec.com)

- SpamKiller (from McAfee, www.mcafee.com)
- MailWasher (free version or Pro version, from www.mailwasher.net)

Any of these programs will go a long way toward reducing the number of spam messages you are forced to handle manually. Especially as the most flagrant spammers change their domain names and hosting Internet Service Providers, and develop new techniques to avoid detection, you may find the low cost of these programs to be a real bargain.

Here are some lesser-known products you may also want to consider:

- SpamNet (www.cloudmark.com)
- FilterPak (www.s4f.com)
- SpamFilter (www.spamfilter.com)
- Spam Inspector (www.giantcompany.com)

This is also a popular category for shareware authors to devote their efforts. A recent search on Tucows.com listed some 50 shareware and demo programs to filter spam, and a Google search reveals thousands of "hits" on this subject.

# Chapter 10
## Other Forms of Malware

In addition to viruses and spam, there are other categories of messages that can cause various types of problems. This chapter will discuss some of those malevolent pieces of software and the grief they may cause, along with some examples that might have appeared on your computer at one time or another.

On the lighter side of this whole issue, this chapter will conclude with the category "When Not To Worry." If you need a chuckle, or a break from the heaviness that permeates most of this book, you might want to skip to the last few pages of this chapter now!

These are the other forms of malware that will be covered in this chapter:

1. Adware
2. Spyware
3. Pop-Ups and Pop-Unders
4. Backdoors
5. Key Loggers or Keystroke Recorders
6. Browser Hijackers
7. Phishing Expeditions
8. Parasiteware
9. Scumware
10. Time Wasters
11. Hoaxes and Urban Legends

## Adware

Adware refers to any unsolicited advertising message found on or associated with a Web page you are viewing. Here is a concise definition of Adware, from www.Whatis.com:

> *Any software application in which advertising banners are displayed while the program is running. The authors of these applications include additional code that delivers the ads, which can be viewed through pop-up windows or through a bar that appears on a computer screen. The justification for adware is that it helps recover programming development cost and helps to hold down the cost for the user.*

While annoying, adware is not malicious and rarely causes serious problems on computers that are delivering such advertising messages. The same can't be said of adware's malevolent first cousin, Spyware.

## Spyware

There are many definitions of Spyware, but this one, from Counterexploitation (www.cexx.org), is among the most comprehensive:

> *Spyware is a generic term typically describing software whose purpose is to collect demographic and usage information from your computer, usually for advertising purposes. The term is also used to describe software that "sneaks" onto the system or performs other activities hidden to the user. Spyware apps are usually bundled as a hidden component in mis-labeled "freeware" and shareware applications downloaded from the Internet – a spyware module may be active on your computer at this moment without your knowledge. These modules are almost always installed on the system secretively, suggesting that spyware companies know how users feel about such software and figure that the best/only way to ensure its widespread use is to prevent the end-user from discovering it.*

While you may like the idea of receiving customized advertising messages, instead of every advertisement a company may have available, spyware at best imposes a burden on your computer and your Internet connection. Running in the background, spyware requires some of the processing power of your computer. That can slow down the things you want to do, like surfing the Internet.

Unfortunately, all spyware isn't programmed to the highest standards. What that means to you is that these programs, running in the background without your knowledge or approval, will sometimes be the cause of system crashes or hangs, or other undesirable behavior. Even if they behave themselves perfectly, the fact remains that you never knowingly invited them into your computer, and they are usually unwelcome guests.

So, how did they get there in the first place? In very much the same way as a Trojan Horse, which was covered in the Definitions in Chapter 4 of this book. You may have clicked on a link in a Web page that offered to speed up your Internet connection, or memorize your passwords for you, or make your outgoing e-mail messages more attractive, or provide some other perceived benefit to you. Such a promise may have induced you to follow the link and, in the process, install the spyware.

It should be noted here that the providers of most of these products would vehemently deny that they are, or contain, spyware. This deniability usually comes down to a difference in interpretation of the meaning of the term. But most of the spyware removal programs will flag these programs as sources of spyware. So, who are you going to believe?

The safest, easiest way to rid your computer of spyware and unwanted adware is to use software intended for that purpose. Three commercial products that provide such functionality are PestPatrol, from PestPatrol, Inc., at www.pestpatrol.com; Spy Sweeper, from Webroot Software, at www.webroot.com; and ZeroSpyware, from FBM Software, at www.zerospyware.com.

There are two widely used freeware programs that do an excellent job of identifying and removing spyware from your system. These are Spybot Search & Destroy, from PepiMK Software, at www.safer-networking.org and Ad-Aware, from Lavasoft, at www.lavasoftusa.com. More recently, Microsoft has entered

**Here are some of the most infamous examples of programs that include spyware. How many do you recognize?**

- Bonzi Buddy
- Comet Cursor
- Gator
- Hotbar
- KaZaA
- SaveNow
- WeatherBug
- Xupiter Toolbar

this field with Microsoft AntiSpyware, which was formerly known as Giant AntiSpyware. You can download a beta (free) version from www.microsoft. com/athome/security/spyware/software.

In looking for software that will remove spyware and protect your computer from becoming infected by such programs, you need to be especially wary of unknown products. There have been several instances of supposed spyware removal programs that are actually spyware themselves. Probably the most egregious example is Spyware Assassin, from MaxTheater Inc.

According to the Federal Trade Commission, free spyware scans offered by MaxTheater turned up evidence of spyware even on machines that were completely clean, and the Spyware Assassin program did not actually remove spyware. A U. S. court recently ordered the company to suspend its activities until a court hearing.

Many articles have been written about spyware and the problems it can cause. At least two widely circulated articles on this subject quote The Virus Doctor, and may provide further information you would find valuable.

The first article appeared in *The Houston Chronicle* and is entitled *Spyware: They Came From Cyberspace*. You can read it at www.chron.com/spyware.

Another article first appeared in the Credit Union National Association member newsletter and has since been reprinted in the newsletters and e-zines of many member credit unions. The original article is available at http://hffo.cuna.org/story.html?doc_id=782&sub_id=12433.

## Cookies – Are They, or Aren't They?

What about cookies? Many people describe cookies as spyware, and encourage you to delete them on a regular basis. In fact, cookies are mostly intended to benefit you and make your Internet surfing experience easier, faster, and more reliable.

Cookies are small files, stored on your computer, that keep track of various things you have done on the Internet. In that respect, cookies are similar to spyware. There are two important differences, though, between these similar but unrelated bits of data.

First, a cookie is not a program; it does not execute programmed instructions and cause your computer or browser to do anything on its own. A cookie merely contains data, which a Web site may interrogate in order to keep you from having to re-enter data that you have already filled in at an earlier time.

Second, cookies are readily accessible to you. Using standard browser and Windows functions, you can see the contents of the cookies and delete any of them that you'd rather not have stored on your computer. There's even an option in most browsers that lets you specify that all cookies are to be deleted every time you exit from the browser.

A legitimate concern about cookies is the fact that some of the information contained in them could be confidential or, at least, sensitive. With that fact in mind, if a hacker gained access to your computer, and, in turn, your cookies, he/she could conceivably upload this information for any purpose they might choose.

In most cases, the likelihood of such an occurrence is so low that deleting the cookies on your computer would cause you much greater inconvenience than any reduction of security risk would warrant.

If you're particularly sensitive about anybody finding out things that might be contained in cookies, or if you're just paranoid, you may delete your cookies any time you wish. You need to understand, though, that some Web sites will not function properly if you block cookies from your computer altogether.

## Pop-Ups and Pop-Unders

Pop-Ups and Pop-Unders are those annoying windows that open when you access a Web page, usually advertising some product that is in no way related to the site you're navigating. Beside the nuisance factor, these extra windows take time to load, especially on a dial-up Internet connection.

Pop-ups and pop-unders also provide another possible entry point for viruses to infect your computer. Like spyware, the best way to rid your computer of these pests is through the use of a utility program.

In most cases, you can block pop-ups and pop-unders without buying any additional software. AOL offers free pop-up blocking, as do many other Internet Service Providers. Another source of free pop-up blocking is the

Google Toolbar, which you can download from www.google.com and install in your Browser.

If your computer is running Windows XP with Service Pack 2 installed, Internet Explorer includes a Pop-up Blocker. This setting is found on the Privacy tab of Internet Options. You can access this feature from Internet Options in Control Panel or from the Menu Bar of Internet Explorer under Tools | Internet Options.

Within the Microsoft Pop-up Blocker, configuration options allow you to specify certain pop-ups that should be allowed, and other personal preferences you may want to customize.

You may still choose to use a third-party utility program to block pop-ups and pop-unders on your computer. Two of the most widely used programs for this purpose are AdSubtract, from Intermute, Inc. at www.adsubtract.com, and Pop-Up Stopper, from Panicware, at www.panicware.com.

If you do choose to block pop-ups and pop-unders, some of the Web sites you access may not function properly; you may need to temporarily enable these programs for some Web pages. Or you may want to add those sites to the list of Allowed Sites if your chosen pop-up blocker offers such an option.

A relatively new form of pop-up has been created to take advantage of a standard feature in Windows 2000 and Windows XP. This type of malware exploits the Messenger Service, which by default is started every time either of these Operating Systems is loaded.

What is particularly irritating about these pop-ups is the fact that they appear on top of whatever is on your desktop at the time, and they cannot be minimized. The screen shot in Figure 10.1 is typical of the messages contained in these Messenger Service windows.

It is important to note that these messages are not related to your Web browser, e-mail program, Windows Messenger, or MSN Messenger. You will probably want to disable the Messenger Service on your computer in order to prevent this type of pop-up.

Turning off the Messenger Service is a two-step procedure. In Control Panel,

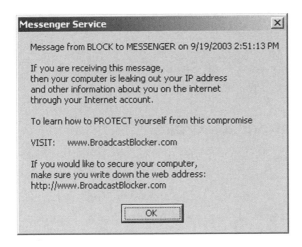

*Figure 10.1*
*This Messenger*
*Service message*
*looks like a*
*Pop-Up, but it*
*really isn't.*

choose Administrative Tools | Services. Scroll through the list of services until you find Messenger, then double-click on that entry.

Slightly below the center of that dialog box, if Service status: is shown as Started, click on Stop. After the service has stopped, change the Startup type to Disabled. That change will prevent the Messenger service from starting the next time Windows is started.

If the Messenger service is already shown as Stopped, you need make no changes in this area. If your computer has Windows XP with Service Pack 2 installed, the Messenger service no longer starts automatically.

## Backdoors

Backdoors are some of the most insidious forms of malware, as they hold the potential to give hackers full access to any files on your computer. They may be installed as part of a virus infection, or may come through spyware, as a Trojan horse. Regardless of how a Backdoor has been installed on a compromised system, it allows a hacker access to that computer without authorization.

The term Backdoor is also used to describe a deliberate, undocumented method of entering a program without going through the normal security procedures, including User ID and Password entry. Software developers frequently use this approach in order to give their programmers easy access to the program for testing and debugging purposes. Such entry points should be removed from the program before it is made available commercially.

An Anti-Virus program is the most effective method of closing any Backdoors on your computer. In conjunction with Spyware removal programs, these "Welcome mats" for hackers can be closed fairly easily.

## Key Loggers or Keystroke Recorders

Key Loggers or Keystroke Recorders are typically installed by Backdoor programs, Spyware, or Viruses. Once installed on a computer, these programs record every key that is pressed on the keyboard of the infected computer. Those keystrokes are saved in a file on the computer, then periodically uploaded to the hacker or Web site responsible for installing or activating the program in the first place.

The purpose of these programs is to look for valuable information, such as credit card numbers, User IDs and Passwords, and information that you may have entered into forms on Web sites. The hackers can then sell this information, or use it themselves for identity theft or other nefarious purposes.

The reason Keystroke Recorders are so dangerous to computer users is the fact that these programs intercept the information directly from the keyboard. Even if you believe your computer is secure, because you use 128-bit encryption or some other form of high-level security, a Keystroke Recorder stores the keyboard input before any encryption takes place.

Like Backdoors, Keystroke Recorders are most effectively detected and removed by your Anti-Virus program and Spyware removal tools.

## Browser Hijackers

Browser Hijackers are programs that make unauthorized changes to your Internet Browser settings, in order to direct you to their advertisers. These changes are typically made to your Browser's Home Page, Default Page, or Search Page. In some cases, these programs will install new Browser Help Objects (BHOs) on your system as well.

If your computer has fallen prey to a Browser Hijacker, you will know it as soon as you open your Internet browser program. If your browser opens to an unfamiliar home page, such as Golden Palace Casino, a pornographic site, or a full-page search screen, that is the behavior that fits into this category.

When you see these symptoms, it is possible that you can reset your Home Page to its original value. In Internet Explorer, click on Tools | Internet Options... and change the Home page contents to the Web site you prefer. Then close and restart Internet Explorer, and see whether the Home page has been changed back to the hijacker's site. If it has been, you'll need to follow the instructions in Chapter 13 of this book to resolve the problem.

Another form of Browser Hijacker is the addition of unwanted toolbars in your browser window. These toolbars are most frequently used to direct the user to a Search page, pornographic sites, or pharmaceutical-ordering sites.

Some of the "well-behaved" toolbars allow the user to toggle them on or off through the View | Toolbars menu of the browser. Many of the more prevalent programs in this category do not follow this standard, though, and will require extra effort on your part to remove them from your system.

Without a doubt, the most annoying Browser Hijackers to appear in the past year are variants of a program named CoolWebSearch. These programs seem to be immune to the most widely used spyware-removal tools and can cause serious degradation in the performance and reliability of computers they have infected.

In order to remove some of the most persistent Browser Hijackers, you may need a program specifically designed to clean up computers that have fallen prey to CoolWebSearch. The most effective program for this purpose is CWShredder, from InterMute, at www.intermute.com/spysubtract/cwshredder_download. html.

Another program that can be very helpful in finding and repairing hijacked home pages is Hijack This, from Merijn, at www.merijn.org/files/hijackthis. zip. Like CWShredder, this is a free download, but the author will gratefully accept donations for his software.

## Phishing Expeditions

One of the newest forms of malware, and one of the most commonly encountered, is known as "Phishing." This is an approach used by the criminally inclined who are trying to gather information that would be useful for identity theft. They attempt to do so by sending large volumes of misleading e-mail messages to would-be victims.

These e-mail messages are designed to mislead the recipient into believing they come from their financial institution, or credit card issuer. They will typically use the actual logo, colors, and style of message normally used by the company they claim to represent.

The message will say something to the effect that your account may have been compromised, so it will be necessary for you to confirm your account details by clicking on a link in the message. Doing so appears to take you to their Web site.

In fact, the site that has the form for you to "verify" your account information is completely bogus. It is simply capturing the information entered by gullible users, and selling that information to individuals or organizations who will use it to steal your identity.

Some of the most frequent targets of phishing expeditions are Citibank, Washington Mutual, eBay, and PayPal. An e-mail security company, Mail Frontier, has created a test that you may take in order to determine how "phishing savvy" you are. That test can be found at http://survey.mailfrontier.com/survey/quiztest.html.

In addition to the financial sites targeted by early phising expeditions, at least two new tactics have come into widespread use in 2005. The first of these preyed on people who wanted to help the victims of the Tsunami in the Indian Ocean on December 26, 2004. These messages led to Web sites which accepted donations for those victims, but the contributors became the second wave of victims as their credit card information and their identity was stolen.

Another recent development in phishing scams involves discounted airline tickets. In this approach, you use your favorite search engine to find a bargain on airfares to some intended destination. One of the sites found in the search offers great prices for your itinerary, so you buy the tickets from that site, using your credit card.

Instead of issuing your tickets, that site claims that there was a problem processing your credit card, and you'll need to send a cashier's check to pay for the tickets. Of course, at the same time the site is sending you this rejection message, it is capturing your account information, charging other items to your credit card, and selling your information to would-be identity thieves.

As you've probably already guessed, there are no airline tickets. If you actually send them a cashier's check for those imaginary tickets, you've been had twice!

## Parasiteware

Parasiteware is a relatively new term, which encompasses several of the other forms of malware discussed in this chapter. Here is the "official" definition, from www.parasiteware.com:

> ParasiteWare™ - is technology (including, but not restricted to, browser helpers, browser plug-ins, toolbars and pop ups/sliders) that knowingly or unknowingly undermines or removes another affiliate's ability to compete by changing, intercepting or redirecting an affiliate link. Parasiteware™ may be installed knowingly or unknowingly by the end user, altering their normal web browser functions and/or installing a third party application that works through the user's altered browser.

By this definition, spyware, pop-ups and pop-unders, and browser hijackers would all fall under the category of ParasiteWare. Here again, Spyware removal tools should find and remove all forms of ParasiteWare.

## Scumware

Scumware is another term that has several definitions, depending upon the interests of the individual or Web site using the term. Obviously, none of the definitions are positive toward those who create or benefit from Scumware.

Here is one definition, from www.scumware.com:

> Scumware: Software, scripts or programs that are specifically designed to circumvent or steal revenue and traffic from legitimate web sites. Most scumware is also considered to be spyware since it usually includes programs which transmit your personal information. Scumware is usually installed without consent and bundled with other programs such as popular filesharing programs or Adware.

This definition, and the strong emotions associated with it, affects Webmasters and the owners of commercial Web sites. The term Scumware applies as well to software that redirects Web surfers to "adult content" Web sites. This tactic also generates a strong emotional reaction when it is discussed.

Finally, Scumware is sometimes used to describe Digital Rights Management (DRM), which is a relatively new method of licensing digital information. In some ways, DRM can be thought of as a form of copy protection. In this context, Scumware can disable your programs and files if DRM believes you are not entitled to access these products.

## Time Wasters

Time Wasters are in the eye of the beholder. Anyone who uses the Internet has discovered how easy it is to go from one Web site or page to another, and spend hours of unbudgeted time on-line. Only you can decide what is a waste of time, and what is time spent doing valuable research. But the biggest time wasters are probably the endless e-mail messages from friends, family, and business associates.

We all have them—the people who send us jokes, petitions, warnings, get-rich-quick schemes, and anything else that comes through their e-mailbox. And most of those messages have been forwarded, frequently through several generations of correspondents.

In an ideal world, you could simply ask those people to stop wasting your time with all this foolishness, they would honor your request, and the problem would be solved. But in the real world, it's not always that simple. You may not be comfortable making such a request, or the sender may be someone who would be offended that you don't share their appreciation for these nuggets.

Fortunately, technology provides an alternative that will avoid any confrontation or hurt feelings. Using the standard filtering tools provided by your e-mail program, you may define rules for handling any incoming e-mail from a particular sender's address.

Using Microsoft Outlook Express as an example, Figure 10.2 illustrates the steps for applying Mail Rules to handle this situation.

*Figure 10.2 This Mail Rule causes any messages received from Bozo@clown.com to be moved directly into the Time Wasters folder.*

In Step 1, you describe the Conditions for this rule. In this case you specify, "Where the From line contains people." In Step 3, you identify the name or e-mail address of the sender(s) who are to be covered by this rule.

In Step 2, you specify the Actions for this rule. What should be done with an incoming message that meets the Conditions defined in Step 1? The most common Actions are to delete the message or to move it to a specified folder. In Step 3, you choose the folder to which the message is to be moved.

By applying Mail Rules judiciously, you can eliminate many of the time wasters from your daily Inbox processing. It's sometimes hard to believe the number of messages that end up in the selected folder in a relatively short amount of time.

To be fair, take a look at your own e-mailing habits and be sure you're not one of those people who wastes others' time in this way. If you find yourself reflexively forwarding a high percentage of your incoming e-mail, your recipients would appreciate some restraint on your part!

## Hoaxes and Urban Legends

The final category of Malware we will cover here is Hoaxes, and the closely related category of Urban Legends. These are usually fairly predictable, but it seems that every day, somebody sees one of these chestnuts for the first time. When that happens, they feel compelled to forward it to everyone they know.

Most of these messages fall into one of several broad categories, such as these:

- Computer viruses ("not detected by Norton or McAfee...")
- "Something for nothing"
- "Get-Rich-Quick" schemes, including chain letters
- "Nigerian letters" (or letters from other nations, usually in Africa)
- Threatened government action
- Threats to your physical security or health
- Petitions or moral outrage
- Lost or missing persons, especially children

Most of these categories are self-explanatory, but since this is a book about computer viruses, we will mention by name three of the most frequently repeated virus hoaxes:

- Sulfnbk.exe
- Jdbgmgr.exe
- WTC Survivor

Yes, all three of these are false alarms, but all have been circulating since 2001 (Sulfnbk.exe and WTC Survivor) and 2002 (Jdbgmgr.exe). They are still near the top of the list of most widely forwarded virus hoaxes.

Another virus-related hoax that has been circulating since 1999, claims that you can keep your computer from spreading viruses by inserting an invalid e-mail address as the first entry in your Address Book. No, that technique doesn't work either.

Any time you receive a message on any of these subjects, it's pretty safe to assume it is a hoax. An almost certain tip-off to a hoax is any message that urges you to forward it to everyone you know.

## Checking Out Suspected Hoaxes and Urban Legends

There are a number of sites dedicated to debunking hoaxes and urban legends. Among the most complete and user-friendly is www.snopes2.com; another is www.truthorfiction.com. For supposed viruses, you might want to use the

Search function on your Anti-Virus software vendor's Web site, or go to www.
vmyths.com.

There's actually a Portal, www.purportal.com, devoted strictly to hoaxes and
urban legends. This site includes a meta search capability, which allows you
to search for hoaxes through multiple Web sites simultaneously. This portal
also includes links to more than 40 of these sites, as well as numerous articles
about popular hoaxes and scams. If you want a good laugh, check out the
correspondence with the author of a "Nigerian letter."

While most of these hoaxes and Urban Legends are basically harmless, other
than possibly affecting your financial condition, there is one widespread
health-related hoax that could actually cause you to be harmed if you blindly
follow the advice it contains.

## Dangerous Hoax

This is the "Cough CPR" hoax, which has been around for a while but has
made a resurgence in recent months. You may have seen it, and on the surface it sounds reasonable. The message instructs you on a procedure to follow if you recognize that you are having a heart attack, and no medical help
is readily available.

This e-mail directs you to cough vigorously until you can get yourself to a hospital or other medical facility, and offers specific guidelines for the type of
coughing and breathing to do, and the best timing. This guidance is based on
a study that is said to have demonstrated that this technique improves your
odds of survival in such cases.

The only problem is that this technique is only appropriate in some cases,
under close medical supervision. In other cases, or if not applied correctly,
this procedure can cause further damage to the heart muscle, and could even
result in the death of the victim.

In other words, don't follow this advice! And any time you receive this message (it will always be forwarded, of course), you will be doing the sender a
favor, and possibly even saving someone's life, if you reply immediately and let
them know the truth about this dangerous urban legend.

For the full details, if you do a search on any search engine for "cough

CPR", you will find numerous references to it. For possibly the most authoritative and up-to-date discussion of this subject, you may want to go directly to www.americanheart.org, the Web site of the American Heart Association.

## When Not to Worry

Considering all the problems that can be caused by viruses, and the nuisance and inconvenience of hoaxes and urban legends, it's nice to know that there is a lighter side to this discussion. Here are some warnings on various subjects you may receive in e-mail messages, none of which will hurt you. Enjoy!

## The Amish Virus

You may at some time receive the Amish Virus. It contains the following message:

*"Thou hast just received the Amish Virus. Since we are dedicated to "low-tech," and do not have electricity or computers, thou art on the honor system. Please delete all of thy files. I thanketh thee,"* – Abe

## Survey Scam

Here's another one, which arrives in an e-mail message with the Subject: Hoax Warning!

I hate those hoax warnings, but this one is important! Send this warning to everyone on your e-mail list.

If someone comes to your front door and says they are conducting a survey and asks you to take your clothes off, do not do it!!! This is a scam; they only want to see you naked. I wish I'd gotten this yesterday. I feel so stupid and cheap now...

## It Must be True, I Saw it on the Internet

The next time some well-meaning cyber-buddy of yours sends an e-mail suggesting you'll get free shares of stock in a company that is just about to go "public," or warning you of a dreaded disease being spread via hat pins left on movie theater seats you may want to reply with a link to this page.

The following story is a montage of several of the urban myths currently floating around cyberspace. This anonymous email is being passed around under the heading, "It Must be True, I Saw it on the Internet."

*I was on my way to the Post Office to pick up my case of free M&Ms (sent to me because I forwarded an e-mail to five other people, celebrating the fact that the year 2000 is "MM" in Roman numerals), when I ran into a friend whose neighbor, a young man, was home recovering from having been served a rat in his bucket of Kentucky Fried Chicken (which is predictable, since, as everyone knows, there's no actual chicken in Kentucky Fried Chicken, which is why the government made them change their name to KFC).*

*Anyway, one day this guy went to sleep and when he awoke he was in his bathtub and it was full of ice and he was sore all over and when he got out of the tub he realized that HIS KIDNEY HAD BEEN STOLEN. He saw a note on his mirror that said "Call 911!" but he was afraid to use his phone because it was connected to his computer, and there was a virus on his computer that would destroy his hard drive if he opened an e-mail entitled "Join the crew!"*

*He knew it wasn't a hoax because he himself was a computer programmer who was working on software to prevent a global disaster in which all the computers get together and distribute the $250.00 Neiman-Marcus cookie recipe under the leadership of Bill Gates. (It's true – I read it all last week in a mass e-mail from BILL GATES HIMSELF, who was also promising me a free Disney World vacation and $5,000 if I would forward the e-mail to everyone I know).*

*The poor man then tried to call 911 from a pay phone to report his missing kidney, but a voice on the line first asked him to press #90, which unwittingly gave the bandit full access to the phone line at the* guy's expense. Then reaching into the coin-return slot he got jabbed with an HIV-infected needle, around which was wrapped a note that said, "Welcome to the world of AIDS."

Luckily he was only a few blocks from the hospital—the one where that little boy who is dying of cancer is, the one whose last wish is for everyone in the world to send him an e-mail and the American Cancer Society has agreed to pay him a nickel for every e-mail he receives. I sent him two e-mails, and one of them was a bunch of x's and o's in the shape of an angel (if you get it and forward it to more than 10 people, you will have good luck but for only 10 people you will only have OK luck and if you send it to fewer than 10 people you will have BAD LUCK FOR SEVEN YEARS).

So anyway the poor guy tried to drive himself to the hospital, but on the way he noticed another car driving without its lights on. To be helpful, he flashed his lights at him and was promptly shot as part of a gang initiation.

Send THIS to all the friends who send you their mail and you will receive 4 green M&Ms—if you don't, the owner of Procter and Gamble will report you to his Satanist friends and you will have more bad luck: you will get sick from the sodium laureth sulfate in your shampoo, your spouse will develop a skin rash from using the antiperspirant which clogs the pores under your arms, and the U.S. government will put a tax on your e-mails forever.

I know this is all true 'cause I read it on the Internet.

– Author unknown

## The C-Nile Virus

Here's another one, the C-Nile Virus, which actually affects many computer users:

It seems that there is a new virus called the C-nile Virus that even the most advanced programs from Norton cannot kill:

For some reason, this virus appears to affect only those PC operators who were born before 1958.

Symptoms of C-Nile Virus:

1. Causes you to send blank e-mail
2. Causes you to send e-mail to the wrong person
3. Causes you to send back the message to the person who sent it to you
4. Causes you to send the same e-mail twice
5. Causes you to forget to attach the attachment
6. Causes you to hit "SEND" before you've finished the

## Urgent Virus Warning

Finally, if you want to see just how dangerous a virus infection can be, here's a warning that is making the rounds of the Internet. You may want to pass this along to your friends, coworkers, and correspondents. To make it easier for you to photocopy this warning and distribute it, you will find it in full on the following page.

## URGENT VIRUS WARNING

*If you receive e-mail with a subject line of "Badtimes," delete it immediately WITHOUT reading it. This is the most dangerous e-mail virus yet.*

*It will re-write your hard drive. Not only that, but it will scramble any disks that are even close to your computer. It will recalibrate your refrigerator's coolness setting so all your ice cream melts and milk curdles. It will demagnetize the strips on all your credit cards, reprogram your ATM access code, screw up the tracking on your VCR and use subspace field harmonics to scratch any CDs you try to play. It will give your ex-boy/girlfriend your new phone number. It will mix antifreeze into your fish tank. It will drink all your beer and leave its dirty socks on the coffee table when there's company coming over.*

*It will hide your car keys when you are late for work and interfere with your car radio so that you hear only static while stuck in traffic. It will give you nightmares about circus midgets. It will replace your shampoo with Nair and your Nair with Rogaine, all the while dating your current boy/girlfriend behind your back and billing their hotel rendezvous to your Visa card. It reaches out from beyond the grave to sully those things we hold most dear.*

*"Badtimes" will give you Dutch Elm disease. It will leave the toilet seat up and leave the hairdryer plugged in dangerously close to a full bathtub. It will wantonly remove the forbidden tags from your mattresses and pillows, and refill your skim milk with whole. It is insidious and subtle. It is dangerous and terrifying to behold. It is also a rather interesting shade of mauve.*

*These are just a few signs.*

*Be very, very afraid.*

# Chapter 11
## Anti-Virus and Firewall Software

O f all the steps you can take to secure your computer against viruses and other forms of malware, none are more critical than installing the appropriate protective software. You will certainly need an AV software product, and in most cases a software firewall as well. This chapter will explain the differences, the purpose, and your choices of products in these categories.

## Anti-Virus Software

When it comes to protecting your computer from viruses, there is no shortage of anti-virus software from which to choose. At last count, there were over 40 such products that run in the Windows environment.

The leaders in terms of market share in the United States are Symantec (http://www.symantec.com), with their Norton AntiVirus products, and Network Associates (http://www.mcafee.com), with the McAfee VirusScan product line.

In addition to these well-known anti-virus software packages, here are some of the other established companies in this industry, and the products they offer:

- Computer Associates (InoculateIT, eTrust),
  http://www.ca.com/etrust
- F-Secure (F-Secure Anti-Virus), http://www.f-secure.com
- FRISK Software International (F-Prot Anti-Virus),
  http://www.f-prot.com
- Kaspersky (Kaspersky Anti-Virus), http://www.kaspersky.com/
- Panda (Panda Antivirus), http://us.pandasoftware.com/
- Sophos (Sophos Anti-Virus), http://www.sophos.com/
- Trend Micro (PC-cillin), http://www.antivirus.com/

For a more extensive list, see Microsoft KnowledgeBase Article #49500. The most recent revision of this article lists 21 vendors of anti-virus software. The full article can be found at http://support.microsoft.com/default. aspx?scid=kb;en-us;49500.

Another article on the Microsoft Web site lists "Microsoft Antivirus Partners," with 25 companies listed. This article is at www.microsoft.com/security/partners/antivirus.asp.

Another listing of AV software products is offered on the Web site of Virus Bulletin, at http://www.virusbtn.com/vb100/archives/tests.xml?200406. This site lists most of the popular (and some not-so-popular) products and shows the results of the tests they performed on each program. Some of the results may be different from what you would expect.

## Free Anti-Virus Software

If you are faced with an extremely limited budget, or if you haven't yet had the occasion to see first-hand the extent of damage that a virus can cause, you may be inclined to use a free anti-virus program.

There are several ways you can use anti-virus software without paying for it. For the really brave (some would say "foolhardy"), there are shareware AV programs you might want to consider. This book will not provide any recommendations for AV software in this category.

A more palatable alternative would be to choose the trial version, or the free version, of an established AV program. Several vendors offer their product free of charge for home or non-commercial use. In alphabetical order, these are the most popular:

- Alwil (Avast!), http://www.avast.com/
- Grisoft (AVG Anti-Virus), http://www.grisoft.com

Some of the other AV software vendors offer trial periods of their commercial products, which is a good way for you to try those products before paying for them. These trial periods may be quite generous, running from 30 days to 12 months.

The following link, to the Microsoft Web site, lists six introductory offers for anti-virus software, from six of the vendors listed above: http://www.micro-soft.com/security/protect/windowsxp/antivirus.asp

## On-Line Virus Scans

The final method of scanning your computer for viruses without paying for any anti-virus software is to run an on-line scan. Several of the major AV software vendors offer that capability from their Web sites. Here are three sites that will perform an on-line virus scan on your computer, free of charge:

- http://www.symantec.com/cgi-bin/securitycheck.cgi – click on "Virus Detection"
- http://housecall.trendmicro.com
- http://us.pandasoftware.com – click on "Panda ActiveScan"

There may be a "catch" to these free scans, though. While all of them will advise you of any virus activity they detected during the scan, they typically will not repair the damage and remove the viruses they found. For that, you may need to buy their program.

While the appeal of no-cost virus scanning is undeniable, the results cannot be as thorough as would be accomplished by running an AV program that is installed on the computer in question. The difference is the inability of any on-line scan to detect viral processes that are presently running on an infected computer.

A viral process refers to the program that is running to cause the virus to reproduce, and to harvest e-mail addresses, delete or modify files, or whatever the payload of that specific virus might be. An on-line scan usually isn't able to dig deeply enough into the computer it is examining to detect viral activity that is already in place and active.

On-line virus scanning will examine the files on the hard drive of the computer in question, and in most cases will be able to identify files that are infected by known viruses. So, running an on-line virus scan periodically is better than no virus protection at all. But this approach can never be as complete as running an AV program that is installed locally on each individual computer.

## Only One Anti-Virus Software Product Per Computer

When you have decided on the AV software that will be installed on your computer, it is critically important to avoid a common temptation. That is to assume that, if one AV software product is good, two must be better.

For maximum protection, only one AV program should be installed on each computer. If there is more than one, the conflicts caused by those competing products can negate each other's effectiveness. While the two AV programs are fighting among themselves, a virus could slip through undetected.

There is nothing wrong with having AV protection on your e-mail server and on each workstation. There is also no problem if your ISP scans all e-mail messages for viruses before sending the message on to the recipient (in this example, you).

The point is that multiple AV products and scans will not cause any conflicts, just so long as those products are installed on different computers or different network segments. In fact, it is advisable to protect every layer of the network from virus infiltration if possible.

### Settings and Options Within Your AV Software

Regardless of the AV software you choose to use, you need to familiarize yourself with the features and options of that product. Specifically, these are the areas that require your attention and possible changes to the default settings for that program:

- Set the program to scan all incoming e-mail and attachments automatically.

- Know how frequently the virus definitions are updated, and the procedure you need to follow in order to keep the definitions up to date.

- Note that, in the case of Norton AntiVirus and McAfee VirusScan, the virus definitions are normally only updated once per week; if you want more frequent updates, you may need to manually download and apply them.

- If your AV program offers the ability to apply updates automatically, be sure that option is enabled.

- Perform a manual update periodically, to catch those changes that were not applied through the automatic update process.

- If your AV software provides for heuristic detection of new viruses, be sure that feature is enabled.

## Software Firewalls

The field of software firewalls isn't nearly as crowded as that of anti-virus software, but there are a number of credible products from which to choose. Not coincidentally, some of the most popular software firewalls come from the same vendors who provide AV software. Indeed, some AV software comes packaged with a firewall.

The three leading examples of such packages are offered by three of the vendors already mentioned above. Here are their products, for the small office/home office (SOHO) environment:

- Norton Personal Firewall, also included in the Norton Internet Security package, from Symantec, at http://www.symantec.com/smallbiz/npf/

- McAfee Internet Security Suite, from Network Associates, at http://us.mcafee.com/root/package.asp?pkgid=144&cid=10353

- Panda Platinum Internet Security, from Panda Software, at http://us.pandasoftware.com/products/platinum_is/

## Free Firewall Software

As with AV software, there are free software firewalls that may be all you need. The leading example is ZoneAlarm, from ZoneLabs (www.zonelabs.com), and this product definitely is worthy of your consideration.

ZoneLabs also offers paid versions of the product with additional capabilities, so take a look at the specifications and decide which version best fits your needs. But even the free version is a full-featured firewall, appropriate for the SOHO market.

Another free firewall worth considering is the Sygate Personal Firewall Standard, from Sygate, at http://soho.sygate.com/products/spf_standard.htm. Like ZoneLabs, Sygate also produces higher-end firewalls for a correspondingly higher price. But the free version may be all you need.

The most popular free firewall software these days is the Internet Connection

Firewall (ICF) that comes as a standard feature of Microsoft's Windows XP Operating System. Whether you are using the Home Edition or the Professional version of Windows XP, this firewall program is included.

While the initial version of ICF was not as full-featured as the other products listed in this section, it did provide some basic protection against viruses such as the Blaster and Sasser worms, and later ones such as the Gaobot family of viruses. The latest version of ICF, which is included in Windows XP Service Pack 2, is far more robust in its capabilities, and may be an acceptable replacement for the third-party firewall software listed in this chapter.

Even if you decide you're not comfortable using free software for such a critical function, buying a software firewall won't break the bank. The SOHO versions of all of these programs are well below U.S. $100, which is a very nominal investment for the protection they offer.

Regardless of the choice you make for a software firewall, one of the same caveats applies as was previously covered with regard to AV software—only one such program should be running on a given computer at a time.

# Chapter 12
## Reading E-Mail Headers

When an e-mail message is sent from one computer to another, that message never goes directly from the sender's computer to that of the recipient. The message must pass through multiple mail servers and possibly other switching, routing, and protection, validation, and relay stations along the way.

At a bare minimum, there will be four waypoints from the initial creation of an e-mail message until it reaches the recipient at the destination computer. Here is the simplified sequence of the message flow:

1. The message is composed on the sender's computer

2. From there it goes to the mail server on the sending end—an Internet Service Provider or a corporate mail server

3. Thence to the mail server at the recipient's end

4. And finally, to the recipient's computer

Again, this sequence of four computers represents a best-case scenario. The architecture of the Internet and the e-mail system will frequently require that a message be passed through multiple mail servers along the way to its ultimate destination.

In addition to the various servers that may be involved, the sender and receiver will frequently have additional equipment that further complicates the issue. Hardware firewalls, routers, and gateways will frequently come into play.

To allow for all of these variables and the constantly changing nature of the Internet and its associated mail servers, each message is preceded by the information that is required in order to guide the message to its intended destination. That information is contained in multiple lines of text, referred to as e-mail headers.

Most e-mail messages that contain spam or viruses can be readily identified by examining the contents of those headers. These headers, while normally not visible to the e-mail recipient, provide valuable insight into the actual identity of the sender.

A detailed discussion of all possible headers and their meanings is beyond the scope of this book, and, frankly, would be pretty boring to the average computer user. Heady stuff for the geeks of the world, but a real yawner for most of the general public.

If you really want to learn more about the intricacies of e-mail headers, there is an excellent, and readable, discussion at http://www.stopspam.org/email/headers.html. The remainder of this chapter will focus on the parts of the Internet headers that you can use to help you recognize suspicious e-mail messages.

## How To See The Headers

Every e-mail program gives the user the ability to examine the header fields, although exactly what you can see in these headers will vary substantially from

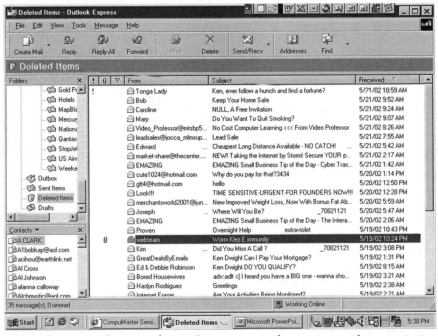

*Figure 12.1 A collection of e-mail messages with suspicious characteristics.*

one such program to another. The following example is based on Microsoft's Outlook Express, which is the most widely used program of this type.

The screen shown in Figure 12.1 illustrates a typical list of e-mail messages received in Outlook Express, with one message selected. The highlighted message appears to come from "Webteam," the Subject is "Worm Klez.E immunity," and it includes an attachment.

To learn more about this message, right-click on it and choose Properties. This action takes us to the screen shown in Figure 12.2.

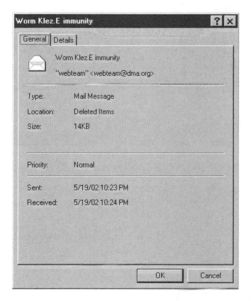

*Figure 12.2 The General tab is the starting point for our analysis.*

On the General tab, you will notice that the "From" address now includes in brackets the actual e-mail address from which this message was sent. Or does it? This message appears to have been sent from dma.org, which is the respected Direct Marketing Association. But we can't take this entry at face value, as it can be easily "spoofed" by spammers or virus writers.

To see a more reliable indication of the actual source of this message, click the "Details" tab of the above dialog box, and you see the screen in Figure 12.3.

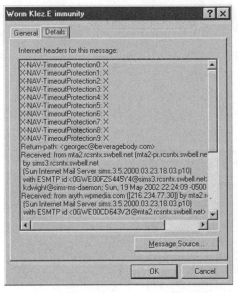

*Figure 12.3*
*The Details tab reveals*
*the Internet headers for*
*this message.*

This screen reveals all the Internet headers for this message, and may provide numerous clues that everything about the message may not be as the sender represented.

You'll notice something that doesn't look right, as soon as you start going through the information on this page. The "Return-path" entry contains a completely different e-mail address from what was shown in the "From" address. You would normally expect both of these entries to be the same, as well as certain other entries that may appear in the e-mail headers.

In this case, the Return-path is shown as georgec@beveragebody.com, which bears no resemblance to the From address of webteam@dma.org. Something is suspicious here! To find out more about this message, let's click on "Message Source...," which gives us the screen shown in Figure 12.4.

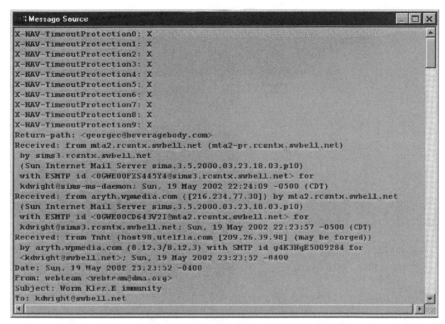

*Figure 12.4 Clicking on the "Message Source" button shows the entire contents of the message, including its Internet headers, without actually opening the message.*

The actual sequence of mail servers through which this message has passed begins at the bottom and works upward. You'll notice that the bottom entry shows "Received: from Tnht ..." and concludes with the entry "(may be forged)." In other words, the first mail server that received this message determined that something about the message didn't appear to be as represented, thus it appended this warning message.

At this point, we know that this messsage is highly suspicious, and opening it could be dangerous. Instead of actually opening the message, we can read its contents by scrolling down farther into the Message Source.

Figure 12.5 shows the actual text of the message that was included in this e-mail.

<FONT>Klez.E is the most common world-wide spreading worm.It's very dangerous by corrupting your files.<br>

Because of its very smart stealth and anti-anti-virus technic,most common AV software can't detect or clean it.<br>

We developed this free immunity tool to defeat the malicious virus.<br>

You only need to run this tool once,and then Klez will never come into your PC.<br>

NOTE: Because this tool acts as a fake Klez to fool the real worm,some AV monitor maybe cry when you run it.<br>

If so,Ignore the warning,and select 'continue'.<br>

If you have any question,please <a href=3Dmailto:webteam@dma. org>mail to me</a>.</FONT></BODY></HTML>

*Figure 12.5 This is the actual text of the suspicious e-mail message.*

In fact, if we had opened this message and selected 'continue' as directed in the message, the Klez virus would have attempted to infect this computer. This message, with the Subject of "Worm Klez.E immunity," is intended to give the recipient the impression that following these instructions will protect him/her from the Klez virus. The actual effect, though, is the exact opposite. Gotcha!

# Chapter 13
## Preventive Measures

In order to understand the preventive measures you may need to take in order to be fully protected from viruses and other forms of malware, you first need to understand the various layers of protection that may be involved in malware defense.

There are actually seven separate stages that must be traversed by any virus, hacker, or other undesirable element. It is possible to intercept the intruder at any of these levels and thus prevent the undesired behavior. These are the stages:

1. The Internet
2. Your Internet Service Provider
3. A hardware firewall
4. A software firewall
5. A locally-installed anti-virus program
6. The Operating System, Internet Browser, and E-mail program on your computer
7. Choices and decisions made by the computer user

## The Internet

At the top level of this hierarchy sits the Internet itself. Individual users or organizations have little control over the protection that may be afforded at this ultimate source of malware attacks, but that would be the logical starting point to prevent these problems in the first place.

## Your Internet Service Provider

Your Internet Service Provider, or ISP, can be a great ally in protecting your computer system from malware. Many of the better ISPs offer virus scanning as a standard component of their service to their subscribers, which is a significant benefit if you're trying to choose among competing ISPs. Some also include spam filtering, ad blocking, and similar services that greatly reduce your exposure to undesirable messages.

If your ISP does provide such services, their efforts are not a substitute for your own security measures. Some of your exposure could occur in ways that your ISP's scanning or filtering procedures may not intercept. Most ISPs that offer this protection also caution you that you are ultimately responsible for the security of your own computer.

# A hardware firewall

The next layer of possible protection comes with installing a hardware firewall. This piece of equipment is standard in the corporate environment, especially where a Wide-Area network or a Virtual Private Network is installed. A hardware firewall is less common in small businesses or home office settings.

## A router functioning as a firewall

If you have a hardware router allowing multiple computers to share a single high-speed Internet connection, such as DSL or Cable service, this device may also serve the same function as a hardware firewall. Let's look at the purpose of each of these devices, and see where their functionality overlaps.

The basic purpose of a router is to connect two separate and unrelated networks. In the case of a small business or home office, the Internet connection via the high-speed DSL or Cable modem represents one of those networks.

The other network in this configuration is the Local-Area Network that connects the computers in the home or small business. The router provides connectivity between the LAN and the Internet, thus allowing all computers on the LAN to share the high-speed Internet connection.

The primary function of a hardware firewall is to prevent unwanted traffic from coming into the attached computers, and to prevent unauthorized traffic from being sent by any computer on the network. The incoming attacks are avoided by making the LAN invisible to the Internet, which is also accomplished by using a router.

When a router is installed between the Internet connection and the LAN, the only address presented to the Internet is that of the router. Since the router in this example is not a computer with an Operating System and software applications running on it, there is no damage that can be caused by a virus or hacker who sends a malevolent message to that address. Thus, the router serves the function of a hardware firewall as well.

## A software firewall

If you're not using a hardware firewall or router, you may want to install a software firewall to serve a similar, if more limited, function. Software firewalls are inexpensive, especially at the small office/home office level, and one of the most widely used software firewalls is available free of charge. Some specific products are discussed in Chapter 11 of this book.

## A locally-installed anti-virus program

Regardless of any other hardware or software you use to protect your computers from harm, it is essential that every computer has a modern anti-virus program installed and running continuously to detect attempted intrusions.

It's critical to note that simply running an anti-virus program, even a very good one, is not sufficient protection against the threats in today's computing environment. Chapter 11 of this book includes a summary of the major programs in this category, which can help you decide which one to use on your computers.

There are two additional steps you will need to take, after you've decided on the specific anti-virus program you will use:

1.  Keep the virus definitions up to date.
2.  Enable automatic scanning of all incoming e-mail messages and attachments.

In most cases, you'll want to configure the anti-virus program to automatically check for updates and download them on a scheduled basis. This schedule should be set for at least once per week, and also allow for unscheduled updates in case of a major virus outbreak.

## Your Operating System, Internet Browser, and E-mail program

The Operating System in use on your computer is the last line of defense against outside forces that would try to make your life miserable. This term will usually refer to some version of Microsoft Windows, but other Operating Systems in use today include Apple's Mac OS, various versions of Unix and Linux, and mainframe Operating Systems as well.

The scope of this book is to provide complete coverage of the multiple versions of Windows, including Windows 95, 98, and ME, as well as NT, 2000, and XP. While there may be some computers still running Windows 3.x, they are not likely to be exposed to the Internet, e-mail programs, or other common sources of virus infection.

## Choices and decisions made by the computer user

In this final category, that catchall description can be further divided into two distinct parts. The first involves settings, options, and standard procedures you will want to use at all times; the second involves a technique known as "social engineering," which is aimed at bypassing the "human firewall," also known as the computer user.

For the top five layers of vulnerability described above, the defensive measures associated with each layer are fairly obvious or explained sufficiently in the preceding text. But the two lowest layers of needed protection involve multiple steps to be taken by the computer user.

The remainder of this chapter will be devoted to specific instructions that need to be followed in order to fully protect your computer from viruses, hackers, and the other forms of malware that could ruin your whole day.

For ease of reference, these steps are numbered sequentially. The steps are listed first, followed by a more detailed discussion where necessary. Steps 1 through 14 apply to the Operating System, and Steps 15 and 16 relate to the Internet Browser and e-mail program in use:

1. *Upgrade Windows to 98 or later.*

2. *Apply all Critical Updates and Security Updates to Windows and Internet Explorer as soon as Microsoft releases them.*

3. *Configure your Operating System to check for Critical Updates every time Windows starts.*

4. *If you have no need to share files or printers, remove the File and Printer Sharing Service* if possible, through the Network Properties.

5. *If you need to have the File and Printer Sharing Service installed but have no need to share files or printers, deselect "I want to be able to give others access to my files"* in Network Properties.

6. *Share folders only if necessary.*

7. *Never share the Root Directory of the C: Drive.*

8. *Set shared access to Read-Only* unless you intend to give another user on your local-area network the ability to change, rename, or delete the shared files.

9. *Require a password for access to shared files and folders.*

10. *Prevent a shared folder from appearing in a Browse window* on another computer on the network.

11. *Clean up programs that start automatically when Windows starts.*

12. *Turn off the Windows Messenger Service if not needed.*

13. *Change Windows Explorer options:*
    a. Show all files (including System and Hidden files)
    b. Don't hide extensions for known file types
    c. In Windows 2000 and XP, Display the contents of system folders
    d. In Windows 2000 and XP, don't hide protected operating system files

14. *Consider third-party utility programs such as Goback.*

15. *Upgrade Internet Explorer to Version 6.*

16. *In Microsoft Outlook or Outlook Express, turn off the Preview Pane.*

Here are more detailed instructions for some of these steps:

1. *Upgrade Windows to 98 or later.* Microsoft no longer supports Windows 95 or Windows NT, and neither of these older Operating Systems provide the built-in Windows Update functionality. Older computers running Windows 95 should be updated to Windows 98 Second Edition, and Windows NT should be updated to Windows Server 2003.

2. *Apply all Critical Updates and Security Updates to Windows and Internet Explorer as soon as Microsoft releases them.* In most cases, the computer user can block malware at the Operating System level by taking this important step. In Windows 98, ME, or 2000, when you click on the Start button, you will see a selection for "Windows Update;" in Windows XP, it may be necessary to look in "All Programs." Clicking on that choice will guide you though the simple procedure to find and apply all Critical Updates and Security Updates that your computer requires.

3. *Configure your Operating System to check for Critical Updates every time Windows starts.* In Windows 98 or ME, download and install the Critical Update Notification feature, which will notify you when Critical Updates are available.

   In Windows 2000 or XP, you may choose to have all Critical Updates downloaded automatically. The latest updates to Windows 2000 and XP also provide the option to install the updates on a scheduled basis, as frequently as every day.

7. *Never share the Root Directory of the C: Drive.* If you must share data from the computer in question, share only the folders that contain files which need to be shared. As a general rule, the safest approach is to share only the My Documents folder, and include other folders under this branch of the directory tree.

   There may be specific programs on a given computer that expect their data files to be in a particular path that does not fall under the My Documents folder. In these cases, you will want to share those folders separately, assigning them a different drive letter from that used for the shared My Documents folder.

10. *Prevent a shared folder from appearing in a Browse window* on another computer on the network. You can accomplish this objective

by ending the folder name with a $ (Dollar sign) when you assign the shared name for the folder. For example, assign a shared name of C:\ Payroll$ to the C:\Payroll folder.

When the folder is shared with this name, another user on the network can double-click on the icon for this computer but will not see the Payroll folder listed as a shared resource. But if that user knows the name of the shared folder, he/she will have access to it by using the Universal Naming Convention (UNC), e.g. \\computer\folder$.

11. *Clean up programs that start automatically when Windows starts.* This step is most easily accomplished in Windows 98, ME, and XP through the use of the Msconfig utility. With the older versions of Windows, including Windows 2000, it may be necessary to manually edit the Registry in order to reach this goal.

    The objective of this step is to prevent loading any programs at Windows startup time that launch or reinstall a virus. By investigating each of the programs and processes that start automatically, you will be able to more easily recognize an intruder that is added to the startup sequence as a result of a virus infection.

12. *Turn off the Windows Messenger Service if not needed.* This feature, found in Windows 2000 and XP only, is frequently used to broadcast spam messages. Unless you actually need this service running on your computer, deactivate it through the Administrative Tools in Control Panel.

    Under Administrative Tools, double-click on Services, then find "Messenger Service" in the list of services that appears. Double-click on this service, and in the dialog box that appears, find "Service status." If that shows "Started," click on Stop.

    When the Messenger Service is stopped, change the Startup type to Manual or Disabled. Unless your computer is part of a large corporate network, you probably don't need this service to be running at all.

14. *Consider third-party utility programs such as Goback.* There is a category of utility programs that can revert your computer to its state as of a previous date and time, and thus undo the damage caused by viruses or other unintended actions. This rollback capability goes beyond that

offered by the System Restore function of Windows ME or XP; while System Restore only backs up system files, these third-party programs track changes to any files and folders on the subject computer.

The most common example of programs in this category is Goback, from Symantec. This program was originally developed by Adaptec, which became Roxio and is now included in the Norton SystemWorks package. If your computer is running Windows XP, be sure the version of Goback that you install is compatible with your Operating System, and disable the Windows XP System Restore.

15. *Upgrade Internet Explorer to Version 6.* If you've kept your Windows Updates current, Internet Explorer has already been upgraded to Version 6. Earlier versions of the Microsoft-provided Browser contain significant vulnerabilities that have been exploited by many virus writers.

Outlook Express will normally be updated as well, when Critical Updates for Internet Explorer are applied. To be on the safe side, you can click on Help in Outlook Express and verify the version that is presently running on your computer.

If you're using Microsoft Outlook as your e-mail program, it's important to note that the Windows Update doesn't apply Critical Updates to Microsoft Office components, including Outlook. You'll need to manually check for Office Updates periodically, to ensure that your version of Outlook is protected against vulnerabilities that have been discovered and fixed since the program was first installed on your computer.

16. *In Microsoft Outlook or Outlook Express, turn off the Preview Pane.* Many of the newer generation of viruses infect the target computer as soon as the message that contains the virus code is opened. If your e-mail program uses a Preview Pane, the selected message is opened automatically.

In order to prevent this exposure, it is necessary to eliminate the Preview Pane from your e-mail display. In Outlook Express, this setting is found under the View menu, under Layout... In the lower half of this dialog box, simply un-check the box that says, "Show preview pane."

In Microsoft Outlook, there is a similar entry, directly under the View menu. The "Preview Pane" entry is a toggle, which you turn on and off by clicking this selection.

Netscape Mail has a similar option, as do some other e-mail client programs. While the vulnerability with these other programs is not as pronounced as with Outlook and Outlook Express, the safest approach is to remove this feature from any such program.

The remaining preventive measures fall into the category of "human firewall" issues. In other words, these are behaviors by the computer user that will prevent viruses from being able to infect your computer.

1. *If a message appears suspicious, check out questionable keywords on your Anti-Virus software vendor's Web site; if that search doesn't reveal anything but you're still suspicious, try a Google search or your preferred search engine.*

2. *When in doubt, delete suspected virus messages without opening or reading them.*

3. *Remember that in order to be able to delete messages without opening, you must be sure the Preview Pane is turned off.*

4. *Don't open e-mail attachments from senders whose names or e-mail addresses are not familiar to you.*

5. *Don't open attachments from known correspondents until you verify that the supposed sender actually sent the message and the attachment.* When in doubt, a quick call or e-mail message to the sender may set your mind at ease.

6. *Don't open attachments that were forwarded to you by someone other than the original author.*

7. *Recognize the file types that are most likely to contain viruses.* In order for a virus to do its damage and to spread to other computers, the file attachment must be of a file type that causes instructions to be executed when the file is opened. There are more than 40 file types, or extensions, that include that capability.

Here are the "top 10" file extensions most frequently used by virus-infected e-mail attachments:

.bat
.com
.cpl
.eml
.exe
.pif
.reg
.scr
.vbs
.zip

You will notice that .com is a type of executable file, not just the suffix for an Internet Domain. At least one widespread virus, MyParty, used this ambiguity to deceive recipients into opening the attachment. The text of the e-mail message referred to photos taken at a party, and directed the addressee to click on "my Web site," which had a suffix of .com. Instead of taking the user to a Web site, clicking on that .com file caused the virus to infect the user's computer.

A complete listing of the executable file types is included in Appendix B of this book.

8. *Download files and attachments to a removable input/output device instead of directly to the hard drive of your computer.* This procedure requires additional steps and is not as efficient as downloading directly to the hard drive, but it may be worth the extra effort in return for the reduced exposure to viruses.

   This approach is practical with some devices, but not others. The ideal devices for direct downloads are removable media with reasonable capacity, such as a Zip drive, a USB RAM drive, or a removable hard drive. A floppy disk drive is less desirable, both because of the limited capacity and the relatively slow speed of writing to the diskette. Although a recordable CD may seem like a good choice, software and timing issues make this an unreliable medium for direct downloads.

9. *Don't follow Web links in unsolicited e-mails.* Even if a hyperlink in an unsolicited e-mail message appears to go to a trusted site, it is relatively easy for the virus writer to route that link to a site completely unrelated to the address that appears in your e-mail window.

10. *Don't trust messages in the headers or the last few lines of text in incoming e-mail that indicate the message has been scanned for viruses and found to be clean.* Such messages may be legitimate; Hotmail does automatically scan outgoing messages with McAfee Antivirus, and other users or Internet Service Providers may do the same. But it is very easy for virus writers to add such a line to their virus-infected messages, hoping to lull the recipient into a false sense of security.

11. *Don't download any files from public newsgroups (Usenet news).* Any time you need to download an important file, it should be available

from a reputable, trusted site. Downloading from a newsgroup carries an unnecessarily high risk of virus infection.

12. *Keep the Deleted Items Folder of your e-mail program empty.* Some viruses spread by filling your Deleted Items Folder, thus causing a programming error in your e-mail program that can be used to spread the virus.

    Remember, the Deleted Items Folder is intended for emergency use only. In those rare cases where you accidentally deleted a message, this "safety net" gives you the chance to recover those deleted items.

    But this is not the appropriate place to store any messages that you expect to need to access again in the future. If you need to save some messages, create additional folders for those messages and move the messages to those folders instead of deleting them.

    There is no practical limit to the number of folders you can create, to save messages in any way that is usable to you. For example, you may define a Business Folder and a Personal Folder. Under the Business Folder, you may further subdivide that into folders for Customers, Suppliers, Employees, Financial, etc.

    The Personal Folder, in turn, may contain folders for Family, Social, Church, Charity, or any other categories that may be pertinent to your filing needs.

13. *Don't forward jokes, cartoons, petitions, warnings, etc.* Most of your intended recipients already have more than enough incoming e-mail, so they will thank you for your restraint. Besides, a high percentage of those messages are just perpetuating urban legends anyway. Spreading such misinformation will reduce your credibility in the eyes of your friends and clients.

14. *When e-mailing to multiple recipients, don't put their addresses in the To: or the Cc: fields; use Bcc: instead.* Most e-mail borne viruses spread by looking for e-mail addresses on the infected system. When a message goes out with multiple addresses in the To: or Cc: field, all those addresses are visible on the receiving computer. If that computer becomes infected, the virus has easy access to all those addresses, without having to look in the address book of the infected computer.

Most e-mail programs include the Bcc: capability. This abbreviation designates a Blind Carbon Copy, meaning that it goes to multiple recipients without any of them knowing who else received the message. By using this technique, you prevent the virus writers and spammers from having easy access to the e-mail addresses of the recipients.

15. *If you do forward a message, first strip out embedded e-mail addresses.* We've all received them—the e-mail messages that were forwarded from one group of recipients to another, to another, ad nauseum. And at every step along the way, all of those e-mail addresses are being forwarded.

If you really must forward a message like that, please take the extra time to delete those lines that contain the e-mail addresses of the previous recipients. Whether they tell you so or not, they will appreciate your reducing their exposure to all the potential forms of malware.

# Chapter 14
## Recognizing Virus Behavior

There are many symptoms of virus behavior, some more obvious than others. These symptoms can be grouped into three broad categories, as follows.

## Suspicious messages – maybe a virus

The first grouping includes error messages that let the user know there is something wrong with the computer. These errors may be caused by virus or other malware activity, or there may be other reasons for their appearance:

- If the Operating System (Windows) won't start at all, this could be caused by a virus having corrupted the Boot Sector of the Hard Disk Drive.

- Every time Windows starts, you see the message "Please wait while Setup updates your configuration files." This behavior only occurs on Windows 95/98/ME computers, and indicates that a change to the Operating System is in progress.

- Any time a program generates an Illegal Operation, malware is a likely cause. Especially when the Illegal Operation occurs in a module that is not familiar to the user, this behavior is suspicious. If the problem only arises when a screen saver activates, it is even more likely to be the symptom of a malware attack.

- Any unexplained, new error messages could be caused by virus activity; of course, there are also many non-malware related causes of such errors.

## No messages – still could be symptoms of a virus

The second grouping encompasses symptoms that could indicate virus infection, but may simply be the natural result of hardware and software components that don't play well together. While these could be caused by virus infection, in most cases these symptoms warrant further investigation before assuming the worst-case scenario:

- Sluggish performance of the computer is one possible symptom of a virus infection, but more commonly these days the fault is spyware; if malware doesn't appear to be the culprit, there is almost certainly additional software running in the background that is not necessary, and will be found to be the source of the performance degradation.

- If you notice that the Root of the C: drive on your computer is shared, when that had not been the case previously, that undesired sharing could be a symptom of a virus that is giving a hacker access to all the files and folders on your hard drive.

- If you have changed the options in Windows Explorer as suggested in Chapter 13, but subsequently notice that they have been reset to the default values, this change could be a symptom of virus infection.

- If a program that has been running on this computer suddenly turns up missing or not available, that program could have fallen victim to a virus attack. This symptom is particularly suspicious if the missing program is your anti-virus or firewall software.

- If a shared resource, such as a networked printer, is no longer available across the network, a virus could have broken that connection.

- If your hard drive suddenly and unexpectedly fills up, especially with sequentially numbered files that you don't recognize, a virus may have created those files.

- If you receive Post office rejection notices for e-mails you didn't send, it's possible that a virus has infected your computer and is trying to spread to other e-mail addresses it found on your system; it's more likely, however, that the messages were actually sent by another computer that was infected by a virus, and randomly chose your e-mail address as the "From:" address in the infected messages it generated.

- In some cases, you may actually receive an e-mail from your own address, but you didn't send it. As in the previous example, these messages most frequently come from a virus-infected computer other than yours.

## Almost certain symptoms of a virus

The final category almost certainly indicates that the computer exhibiting these symptoms is infected by one or more viruses. Such a computer needs to be disinfected immediately, before the virus can do any more damage or spread to any more computers or networks:

- The previously installed anti-virus program is missing or will not execute
- You are unable to install Anti-virus software
- You are unable to execute Windows utility programs, such as Regedit.exe and Msconfig.exe
- You are unable to open any programs
- The computer can still access the Internet, but not the Web sites of AV software vendors
- The computer can't access the Internet at all
- New windows open on their own, move around, and/or resize
- Multiple program windows open on their own
- Every unread e-mail message receives a reply, as you watch
- The mouse pointer "chases" icons across the screen
- Anti-Virus and/or Firewall icons in System Tray disappear when the mouse pointer is placed over those icons
- Someone else takes control of your computer
- When shutting down the computer, you receive a Sharing message, "There are 1 user(s) connected to your computer," when your computer is not on a network. The message will be similar to the one shown in Figure 14.1.

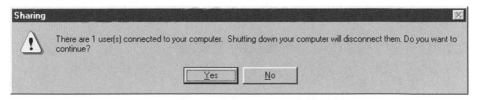

*Figure 14.1 A warning message you may see when you shut down your computer.*

## Sure Signs of Virus Infection

There are times when you will know beyond a shadow of a doubt that your computer has received a virus. In the days when Norton AntiVirus 2001 was the current generation of this popular software product, you'd first see a screen similar to the one shown in Figure 14.2.

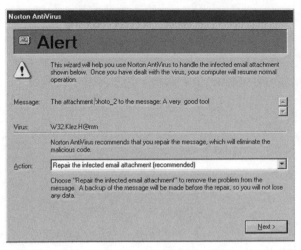

*Figure 14.2 This Alert message from Norton AntiVirus 2001 offers your choice of several possible Actions you may take.*

This message indicates that an incoming e-mail message contained an attachment, in this case photo_2, which was infected by a virus. In this case the virus was the infamous Klez.H worm, officially known as W32.Klez.H@mm.

In most cases, the preferred action when a virus-infected file is identified is to try to repair the damaged file. Since that is the default Action selected in this example, clicking Next > would cause Norton to attempt to repair this attachment.

In many cases, Norton 2001 was not able to repair the virus-infected file, as illustrated by the subsequent screen shown in Figure 14.3. When this situa-

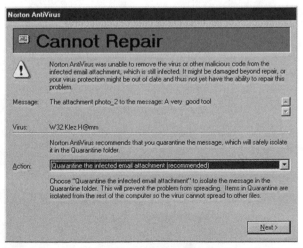

*Figure 14.3 This Cannot Repair message from Norton AntiVirus 2001 offers Quarantine as the recommended Action for you to take.*

tion arises, the second choice of Actions is to Quarantine the infected file, as selected in this example.

Placing an infected file in Quarantine serves two potentially useful purposes. First, it prevents this virus from spreading to other files on your hard drive, or causing any other damage to your computer or your network. This is the most important benefit of isolating the file into the Quarantine folder.

The other reason for placing an infected file into Quarantine is to allow for repair of that file at a later date. Since the virus definitions and automated removal tools are being updated constantly, there's a good chance that a future version of that software will be able to repair damage that can't be handled by the present version.

As a practical matter, in most cases the infected file identified in this message is actually the virus itself, or some related file or folder. If that's the case, your best course of Action is to delete the file instead of leaving it on your computer in Quarantine.

When Norton AntiVirus 2001 had successfully quarantined the infected e-mail message or attachment, it led to the screen shown in Figure 14.4. If you wanted to examine the Quarantine file or delete infected files that had been placed in Quarantine, you could click on the icon to "Run the Quarantine Console now."

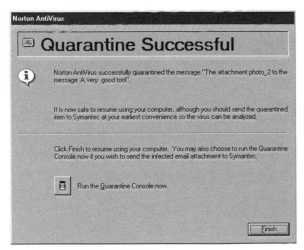

*Figure 14.4 This Quarantine Successful message from Norton AntiVirus 2001 gives you the option to Run the Quarantine Console now.*

The sequence of repair attempts was significantly different in Norton AntiVirus 2002, although the end result is the same. Figure 14.5 illustrates the result of receiving an e-mail message with an attachment that contains the Sobig.F virus.

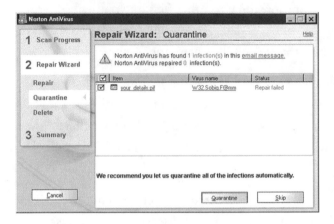

*Figure 14.5 This Repair Wizard message from Norton AntiVirus 2002 offers Quarantine as the recommended Action for you to take, since the Automatic Repair failed.*

When you receive a screen similar to this one, you can click on any of three hyperlinks, underlined and in blue type, to reveal further details. Clicking on the hyperlink to email message at the top of the right-hand pane of this window will provide the details of the message that was infected.

Clicking here will allow you to see the (alleged) Sender's address, the date and time stamp, and other basic information about the message from its headers. Clicking on this link will not open the message, but will show you the relevant contents.

In the center section of the right-hand pane, the Item column contains the name of the infected file. In this case, the infected file was your details.pif, and you can find more details of this file by clicking on its hyperlink.

The Virus name column indicates the name of the virus that infected this file, in this case the infamous Sobig.F, officially known as W32.Sobig.F@mm. Clicking on this hyperlink will take you to the Symantec Web site, and the detailed article about this particular virus or other form of malware.

Finally, the Status column tells us that an attempted Repair of this infected file was unsuccessful. When this occurs, the normal recommendation is that you let the program quarantine the infected file. By clicking on Quarantine, you eliminate this virus-infected file from taking an active role on your computer.

When the file has been successfully Quarantined, you will see a screen similar to the one shown in Figure 14.6.

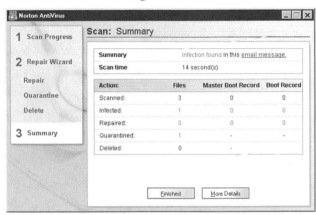

*Figure 14.6 This Scan: Summary screen from Norton AntiVirus 2002 shows the overall statistics on how this virus was handled.*

This screen gives you one last opportunity to review what was found in this specific message, and how Norton handled the virus. Click Finished, and you're done.

Norton AntiVirus 2003 was different from previous versions, both in appearance and in the way it handled virus infections it encountered. Figure 14.7 illustrates the only screen returned for an infection by the Blaster virus/worm.

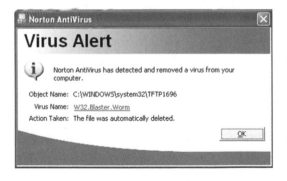

*Figure 14.7 This Virus alert message from Norton AntiVirus 2003 shows that the Blaster Worm was detected and automatically deleted from this computer.*

Here again, clicking on the hyperlink to <u>W32.Blaster.Worm</u> provides the details of this virus infection, from the Symantec Web site.

When Norton AntiVirus 2004 detects a virus in an incoming e-mail message, the program presents a screen similar to the one shown in Figure 14.8.

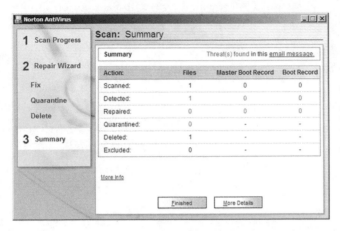

*Figure 14.8 This Scan: Summary screen from Norton AntiVirus 2004 shows the overall statistics on how this virus was handled.*

Clicking on the hyperlink to the email message reveals the details of the infected message, as shown in Figure 14.9.

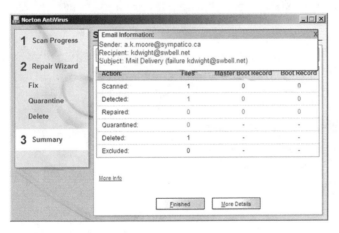

*Figure 14.9 This Email Information pop up screen in Norton AntiVirus 2004 shows the details of the infected e-mail message.*

By clicking on the "More Details" button, you can see the name of the infected file, the name of the threat (the virus, in this example), and how it was handled, as shown in Figure 14.10.

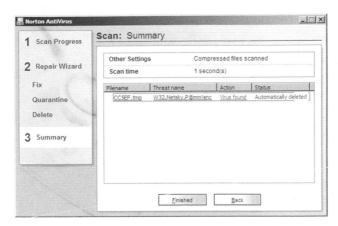

*Figure 14.10 This Scan: Summary screen from Norton AntiVirus 2004 shows the details of the threat(s) detected and their disposition.*

If you want more information on the specific virus found, clicking on the Threat name will take you to the appropriate document on the Symantec Web site. In this case, Norton automatically deleted the infected e-mail message, including the attachment(s). In its place, the user receives an e-mail message similar to the one shown in Figure 14.11.

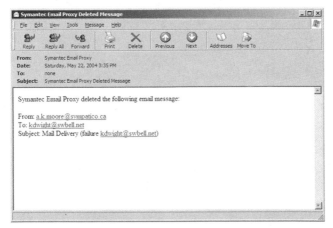

*Figure 14.11 This e-mail message from Symantec Email Proxy provides a permanent record of how Norton AntiVirus 2004 handled an infected e-mail message.*

If your Internet Service Provider provides virus scanning before e-mail messages are delivered to your computer, you will sometimes receive messages similar to the one shown in Figure 14.12.

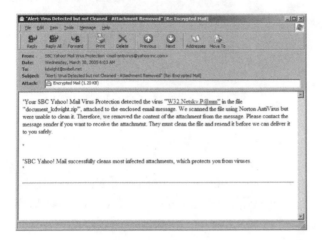

*Figure 14.12 This e-mail message from the recipient's Internet Service Provider is a substitute for an infected e-mail message.*

In this example, the ISP has intercepted an e-mail message that included a virus-infected attachment. In place of the original message, this automatically generated e-mail gives enough information that you may contact the sender if necessary. The infected attachment has been removed from the original message.

## Testing Your Antivirus Protection

With the proliferation of viruses and other forms of malware these days, you should expect to receive notification of attempted virus infection on a regular basis. If your computer doesn't display a warning message from your AV software for a significant length of time (for example, two weeks), it would be prudent for you to test the AV software and be sure it is working properly.

Fortunately, there is an organization that provides a set of anti-virus test files that can be used to verify that AV software is functioning properly. This organization is known as EICAR, which originally stood for European Institute for Computer Antivirus Research.

Their Web address is www.eicar.org , and the About Us page explains that they refer to the organization by its acronym now, instead of its original full name. As explained on the Web site, "...we are now busy in the general IT Security field with a focus on AV and hence we do not refer to the full term anymore."

The test files can be obtained from the following page of the EICAR Web site: http://www.eicar.org/anti_virus_test_file.htm

In describing the purpose of these test files, the Web site defines the individuals and organizations who may have a legitimate need for such a testing environment. Most readers of this book fall into the category described by EICAR as "users of anti-virus software."

Quoting from their Web site, "Using real viruses for testing in the real world is rather like setting a fire to the dustbin in your office to see whether the smoke detector is working. Such a test will give meaningful results, but with unappealing, unacceptable risks."

The Web site provides four separate files that can be downloaded to test your antivirus program in various environments. These files will do no damage to your computer or the files stored on it, but will cause your antivirus program to react as though it had detected a virus in each of the sample files.

If any of these files are successfully downloaded to your computer without your AV program sounding an alert, you know that the program is not serving its intended purpose. The software may be deficient, or it may not be configured properly to detect incoming attempts at virus infection.

## What to Look For if You Suspect a Virus

If you suspect that a virus has infected your computer, here are some steps you can take to confirm your suspicion, or to determine that the cause of the problem lies somewhere other than in the realm of virus-inflicted damage. The exact steps you follow will vary depending upon your Operating System, but this procedure applies to all versions of Microsoft's Windows platform.

### If the computer won't boot

If the computer will not boot into Windows at all, the Boot Sector of your hard drive may have been damaged or corrupted. To determine whether this is the source of your problem, try to boot the computer into Safe Mode. This can be done in either of two ways, but in either case the timing is critical.

When you first turn on the computer, start pressing the F8 key repeatedly until a Boot Menu appears on the screen. Don't hold down the F8 key; just keep hitting it about once every second until the menu appears. If the Windows splash screen appears, that is your indication that you probably missed the "window" of time that the system was looking for the F8 key.

If you do come to the Boot Menu, choose "Safe Mode," and see whether Windows will start in that environment. If it does, that lets you know that your Boot Sector is undamaged, and the problem lies within Windows and its associated programs. At this point, you know the problem requires further diagnosis.

If you missed the Boot Menu, go ahead and restart the computer. You should be able to accomplish this task via the "three-finger salute," or Ctrl+Alt+Del. As soon as you see the black screen, indicating that the computer is restarting, start pressing the F8 key.

The other method, which will take you directly into Safe Mode without going through the Boot Menu, is to press the F5 key as the computer is being powered up, just as described for the F8 key in the preceding paragraphs.

## If the computer will boot into Safe Mode, but not Normal Mode

In this case, the problem is caused by a program or Windows component that is loading automatically at startup time. Safe Mode prevents most of these modules from loading, so your next task is to determine which program is the source of the problem and fix it.

This symptom may be the result of a virus infection, but that will not necessarily be the case. Even if the problem is not virus-related, you still need to resolve the issue, so skip to the section below, "If the computer will boot normally."

## If you never get the Boot Menu, or can't boot into Safe Mode

If the Boot Menu never came up, in spite of your pounding on the F8 key, and F5 wouldn't take you into Safe Mode, then you can assume that the Boot Sector of the hard drive has been damaged or corrupted. Repairing this damage may be fairly simple, or it might require a trained computer technician to make the computer bootable again.

At this point, if you have previously created a Rescue Disk, or a Virus Recovery Disk, or a diskette or CD with a similar name from your AV program, try booting your computer from this disk. In most cases, such a disk will only take you as far as a Command Prompt, but that is at least a starting point for further diagnosis.

If you haven't created such a disk, or if it doesn't work, the final possibility is to boot into a generic Startup Disk for your Operating System. In Windows 95/98/ME, you should have created a Startup Disk when the computer was behaving normally. If you don't have one when you need it, the easiest solution is to find another computer running exactly the same version of Windows, create a Startup Disk on that computer, and use that disk to boot the ailing machine.

For Windows 2000 or Windows XP, you will probably need to boot from the original CD that contains the Operating System. When you do so, one of the options on the Boot Menu is the Recovery Console. This option gives you the ability to restore the Boot Sector, but this is a task that is probably best left to a trained professional.

If you can successfully get to a Command Prompt using one of these methods, your next step is to run a Virus scan from there. In order to do this scan, you will need a command-line version of your AV program, either on floppy disks or a CD. This program is typically found on the Rescue Disk or Virus Recovery Disk referenced above.

If the results of this scan reveal a virus infestation, take those results and proceed to Chapter 15 of this book. Otherwise, the problem is most likely caused by something other than malware. In that case, the solution to the problem is beyond the scope of this book.

## If the computer will boot normally

If the computer boots into normal Windows operation, but you experience symptoms that you suspect to be caused by virus infection, there are numerous steps that may be required to troubleshoot the problem and identify its source.

The first step to take, if possible, is to have your Anti-Virus program scan the entire computer for viruses and other forms of malware. Before initiating the scan, be sure you have updated the virus definitions to the latest version.

If you are unable to automatically update the virus definitions in your AV program, it may be possible to perform a manual update. If you are using Norton AntiVirus, the procedure for manually updating your virus definitions is to use the Intelligent Updater.

To use Intelligent Updater, you will go to http://securityresponse.symantec.com/avcenter/download.html and click on "Download Virus Definitions (Intelligent Updater Only)." This will download an executable (.exe) file that contains all virus definitions as of that date.

If possible, the best way to use Intelligent Updater is to download the file on an uninfected computer and then copy it to a CD or a USB drive. Then take the file to the infected computer and run it there. Double-clicking on the executable file will apply those definitions to the installed copy of Norton AntiVirus.

This procedure does require that the target machine have an installed, working copy of Norton AntiVirus, and a current subscription to the update service. If that is not the case on the infected computer, it will be necessary to reinstall the software and/or purchase a renewal of the update service.

If you are using a different AV software product, its maker may offer a similar provision for performing a manual update of its virus definitions. Check the documentation that was provided with the software, or look on the vendor's Web site to see whether there is an alternative method for updating the virus signatures.

If your AV program no longer appears on the Programs menu, that omission could be confirmation of the presence of a virus. In that case, try to reinstall the Anti-Virus program, but know that you may not be able to do so.

If you are no longer able to run your normal AV program, and are not able to reinstall it, there is another virus scanning program you probably will be able to run successfully. This is a program called Stinger, which you can download from McAfee at http://vil.nai.com/vil/stinger/. You may want to download the program on an uninfected computer and copy it to a CD or USB drive, then run it on the infected computer.

Stinger is not a substitute for a full-time AV program, but it will scan a computer looking for the most common viruses. A recent version included detection for all variants of 47 different viruses, so there is a good chance this simple, free program will detect the viruses that are most likely to have infected your computer.

If you are unable to run any virus-scanning program, a likely cause of that limitation is a program running in the background that is blocking access to most of the common AV software products. Such a program would have been planted and executed by the virus that has infected your computer.

You may be able to work around this behavior by restarting Windows in Safe Mode, and trying your AV program in that environment. If you're not sure how to boot into Safe Mode, that procedure is discussed earlier in this chapter, under the section "If the computer won't boot."

If you are unable to scan for viruses with any AV program installed on your computer, you may be able to do an on-line scan. If you can still connect to the Internet, here are three sites that will scan your hard drive for viruses and report the results to you:

> http://www.symantec.com/cgi-bin/securitycheck.cgi – click on "Virus Detection"
>
> http://housecall.trendmicro.com
>
> http://us.pandasoftware.com – click on "Panda ActiveScan"

Another common symptom of virus infection is the inability to access the Web sites of AV software vendors, so you may not be able to contact any of these sites. If your computer can access the Internet, but not these specific addresses, that is another fairly reliable indication that the machine is, in fact, infected by a virus.

If you can access the Internet, but not the Web sites of AV software vendors, that is a symptom that typically indicates that the virus has modified the HOSTS file on your computer. This file contains information related to specific Web sites, and how to access them. You may be able to solve this problem on your own.

Using the Search or Find option of your Operating System, look for a file named HOSTS. The one you want does not have a file suffix, or extension, and will probably be found in one of the following locations:

C:\Windows – Windows 95/98/ME

C:\Windows\system32\drivers\etc – Windows XP or Windows Server 2003

C:\WINNT\system32\drivers\etc – Windows 2000

When you find the HOSTS file, open it using Notepad. Delete any lines in this file that contain reference to any Anti-Virus, Firewall, or Security software products. Then save the file, close Notepad, and try again to access the site that had been unavailable.

If one of these scans does reveal the presence of a virus, it probably will not repair the damage or remove the virus for you. But it will identify the virus by name, which gives you a good head start on disinfection through other means. Once you have that information, you might want to proceed directly to Chapter 15 of this book.

## Tracking down the culprit

Making the determination as to which program is the source of the undesirable behavior of your computer involves some informed detective work. The exact procedure will vary considerably between different versions of Windows, so they will be presented separately.

In either case, your first step is to close any applications that may be open, then discover what other programs are running without your knowledge. Some of these programs are normal components of your Windows environment, but this is also the hiding place for most forms of malware. Viruses, keystroke loggers, back doors, and some spyware and browser hijackers will reveal themselves in this area.

### Windows 95/98/ME

In the Windows 9x environment, two factors govern the stability of the system and the performance it provides. These elements are (1) the number of programs running in the background; and (2) the percentage of System Resources that are available. To a large extent, these are two pieces of the same puzzle.

There are several ways to determine the System Resources available. Perhaps the easiest is to right-click on My Computer and choose Properties. On the

Performance tab, you'll see an entry showing the percentage of System Resources that are free.

With no applications running, you should see at least 75% free system resources. More is better, but 75% is a reasonable number. If you are seeing less than 50% free before any applications are started, you need to perform some serious surgery in order to make this system stable and reliable.

This figure is inversely proportional to the number of programs running. Accordingly, the most logical way to increase the percentage of free system resources is to reduce the number of programs running in the background.

To see how many programs are running, and which ones they are, you'll need to do a Ctrl+Alt+Del routine. Unlike the earlier Operating Systems, in Windows 9x this procedure will open the Close Program dialog box. Figure 14.13 shows a typical example of what you can expect to see on an uninfected, trouble-free computer.

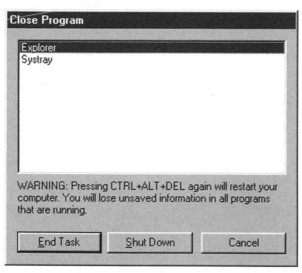

*Figure 14.13 This Close Programs dialog box lists all programs that are presently running on this Windows 98 system.*

This is, admittedly, a very Spartan example of a Windows 9x system. Whereas this screen shot illustrates only two programs running in the background, a more typical example would include at least a dozen entries.

When a Close Program dialog box such as this contains more than ten or twelve entries, the stability of the system and the free system resources are lower than would be considered desirable. Each screen can contain 11 entries, with the last one carried over to the following page.

To quickly calculate the number of programs running in the background when the Close Program dialog box fills multiple pages, just count the full pages, multiply by 10, and add 1. You may be unpleasantly surprised by the number of programs running on the computer that is suspected of being infected by a virus.

To make this calculation more meaningful, it would be helpful to have a baseline number from a time when the computer was performing normally. If you had the foresight to record the names of the programs running at that time, that preparation will greatly simplify the task of recognizing a new program that could be the source of the problem.

Many of the programs that you'll find in the Close Program listing were started automatically when Windows first loaded. Your next task is to examine the list of programs started automatically, and eliminate any that are not necessary. In the process, you could very well stumble across a virus that is the source of the problem.

Windows 98 introduced a very handy utility program that makes it simple and safe for even an inexperienced computer user to find and deactivate programs that start automatically. The program is called Msconfig.exe, and it can be executed from the Run command (click on Start, then Run...). In the "Open" box, type "Msconfig" (without the quotes) and click OK. You'll see a box similar to the one shown in Figure 14.14.

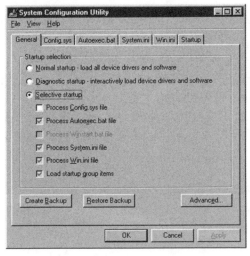

*Figure 14.14 The MSConfig program on this Windows 98 system gives you easy access to programs that are opening automatically when Windows is started.*

Clicking on the Startup tab, you'll see a long list of programs that have been set to load automatically every time Windows starts. Figure 14.15 shows a typical example of a list that might be found on the Startup tab.

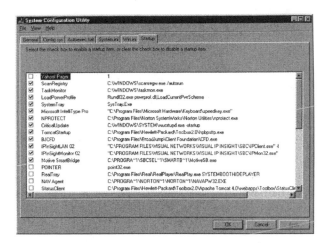

*Figure 14.15 The Startup tab of MSConfig lists the programs that are started automatically as a result of Registry entries in this Windows 98 system.*

If you see any programs in this list that do not need to start automatically, simply click on the box to the left of the program name to remove the check mark. On the other hand, if you see items that are not selected but should be, put a check mark in the appropriate boxes.

Most viruses and other malware will be found on the Startup tab. By removing the check mark from the box, you will prevent that program from starting the next time that Windows loads, but you have not removed the virus from the system.

Furthermore, many modern viruses monitor the status of their entries in this table, and will reinsert themselves after they detect that someone has deactivated them. But at least by finding those programs on the Startup tab, you have identified the source of the problem and can address it more aggressively if necessary.

By default, Windows 98/ME makes six or seven entries to the Startup tab. Here are the program names you will normally find with check marks in their respective boxes:

| | |
|---|---|
| ScanRegistry | Scanregw.exe |
| TaskMonitor | Taskmon.exe |
| LoadPowerProfile | (appears twice) Rundll32.exe Powrprof.dll |
| SystemTray | SysTray.exe |
| SchedulingAgent | Mstask.exe |
| Welcome | Welcome.exe (if the Welcome screen is not disabled) |

In addition to the Startup tab, Msconfig will also show you several additional places where viruses can hide and do their damage out of the light of day. The first area to examine is the System.ini tab.

On this tab, click on the + sign to the left of [boot], and look in this section for an entry that reads "shell=Explorer.exe." If this entry contains any other value, such as Load.exe, this is the "smoking gun" that reveals a virus. Another variation on this technique employed by some viruses is to leave the original entry intact and add an additional entry before or after Explorer.exe.

If the System.ini file appears normal, the next place to look is the Win.ini tab. Click on the + sign to the left of [windows] and look for two entries in that section. These entries are Load= and Run=. If either entry contains a program name after the = sign, verify that the content is legitimate, i.e. that a program by that name should start automatically every time Windows loads on this computer.

Also note that both of these fields may contain multiple entries, and you will need to verify that every entry in both fields serves a desired purpose. These entries are frequently used by printer manufacturers to load their Printer Toolbox into the System Tray at startup time.

Another certain indicator of a virus infection is an entry in the Win.ini file with a value of Load=Wininit.exe. If you see this entry, the computer is infected. You will probably also find a file named Wininit.ini in the C:\Windows folder, which you should delete.

The Msconfig.exe program came with Windows 98 and ME, but did not exist in the days of Windows 95. If you're dealing with a Windows 95 computer, you'll have to find another way to examine and modify these system files.

After you've completed your examination of the System Files as described here, proceed to the section "All versions of Windows," later in this chapter.

## Windows 2000 and Windows XP

These Operating Systems offer numerous hiding places for viruses, spyware, and hackers to lurk and do their damage mostly unnoticed. Flushing them out can involve quite a bit of investigation, but not as much technical expertise as pure patience.

In order to see the list of programs that are running in the background of these Operating Systems, you will need to access the Task Manager. This is accomplished by using the Ctrl+Alt+Del combination of keys.

Figure 14.16 shows a typical example of a Windows Task Manager screen, from a computer running Windows XP.

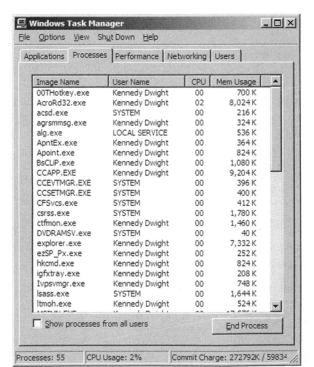

*Figure 14.16 The Processes tab in Task Manager lists all programs that are presently running on this Windows XP system.*

The Applications tab should show no active applications (remember, you want to close all applications before you begin this investigation). The Processes tab is where you will find evidence of virus infection or other malware.

You'll notice that the summary, at the bottom of this screen, contains valuable information. In this example, it reveals that 55 processes are active, which gives you some idea of the scope of the work ahead of you. CPU usage is shown as only 2%, which is a pretty good indication that a virus or hacker is not presently active on this system.

To make the discovery process easier, click on the column heading Image Name. This will cause the entries in this column to be sorted alphabetically, which will facilitate the identification of the various entries.

The objective of going through this list of processes is to identify any that do not belong. In some cases, a virus will clearly and unambiguously identify itself here; for example, the presence of Msblast.exe in this list absolutely tells you that the computer is infected by the Blaster worm.

In the majority of cases, though, the footprint of the malware will not be so readily apparent. The example shown here, with 55 processes presently contained in memory, is fairly typical. At a bare minimum, you can expect to see at least 25 processes on any Windows 2000 or Windows XP system.

The exact processes you can expect to find will vary considerably from one PC to another, depending upon the computer manufacturer and the various hardware devices installed, the software installed, and the Windows services that are active.

You can save yourself a lot of time and effort at this stage by establishing a baseline when this computer is performing normally. By running Task Manager and printing out the results, you will have a record of the Processes that are running when there are no symptoms of virus or other malware infection.

Now, when you do suspect a problem of this nature, your task is greatly simplified. Just compare the list of Processes from the "normal" baseline to those that are active when the computer is exhibiting abnormal behavior.

Most commonly, you will be looking for Processes that were not present in the baseline listing. Any that did not exist on the baseline report but show up in the present listing should be considered suspicious.

At the same time, you want to make sure that certain Processes that were in the baseline listing are not missing from the present list. Specifically, if the processes associated with your anti-virus or firewall software are no longer showing up in the list, you can be fairly certain that the computer has been compromised.

Many of the entries that you'll find in the listing of Processes were started automatically when Windows first loaded. Your next task is to examine the list of programs started automatically, and eliminate any that are not necessary. In the process, you could very well stumble across a virus that is the source of the problem.

Windows XP includes the latest version of the Msconfig program, which was first introduced with Windows 98. This program makes it easy and safe for even a non-technical computer user to identify and deactivate those programs that are starting automatically every time Windows XP opens.

In a puzzling omission, Microsoft did not include Msconfig with any version of the Windows 2000 Operating System. If the computer in question is running Windows 2000, there is no simple, officially sanctioned way to examine and modify the list of programs that start automatically when Windows 2000 loads.

If you're dealing with a Windows 2000-based computer and want to continue this troubleshooting process, proceed to the section "All versions of Windows," later in this chapter.

To use the Msconfig tool on a Windows XP system, click on the Start button, then choose Run... In the "Open" box, type "Msconfig" (without the quotation marks) and click OK. You'll see a box similar to the one shown in Figure 14.17.

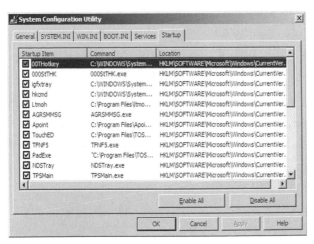

*Figure 14.17 The Startup tab of MSConfig lists the programs that are started automatically as a result of Registry entries in this Windows XP system.*

The Startup tab, shown here, contains the list of programs that have been set to load automatically every time Windows XP starts. You won't recognize many of these program names, so that's where the detective work comes in.

For now, just know that you can prevent any Startup Item in this list from loading automatically, simply by removing the check mark in the box for that item. On the other hand, if you see an entry that is not selected but should be (such as your anti-virus software), click that box to put a check mark into it.

## All versions of Windows

As you look through the Close Program dialog box, or Windows Task Manager, you need to identify the source and purpose of every program or process that is running. There are several methods available to you to meet this goal.

The first step is to compare the list of those items that are running to the list of programs that started automatically when Windows opened. If your version of Windows includes the Msconfig program, the Startup tab is your source of this information.

There are numerous Web sites that provide descriptions and explanations of the programs and processes that may be loaded automatically. Here are three sites you can use for this purpose:

> http://www.answersthatwork.com/Tasklist_pages/tasklist.htm
>
> http://www.kephyr.com/filedb/index/all.html
>
> http://www.windowsstartup.com/wso/browse.php

For any programs and processes that appear in the Close Program dialog box or the Windows Task Manager, but did not start automatically with Windows, probably the most effective way to identify their nature and source is by entering the module name into a search engine, such as Google.

In most cases, such a search will reveal multiple "hits" which will usually show a fairly reliable pattern regarding the nature of that module. For example, if the first page includes five or more entries that reference a virus or spyware in connection with the module in question, you have a strong reason to suspect that program as the source of the problem.

If a Google search doesn't find any "hits" for a particular search, that failure could be a sign that the module is the source of a virus. The reason for this apparent contradiction is the way that some viruses create the file name of the executable file.

A fairly common technique used by many virus writers is to randomly generate a file name for the virus-infected file. Such a file name may be made up of a nonsensical collection of letters and numbers and will be different every time the virus is generated. Thus, the random file names are unlikely to show up in a search across the Internet.

For any programs that are starting automatically, but seem to serve no useful purpose, the obvious next step is to remove them from the startup sequence. If the Msconfig program is available to you, simply remove the check mark from the boxes associated with these programs, restart Windows, and see if the problem is still present when Windows finishes loading.

If the symptoms don't change at that point, check the Task List again and see whether the programs you had deactivated have, in fact, returned and are running again. If so, you can be fairly certain that those entries are viruses, or at least spyware.

# Chapter 15
## What to Do if Your Computer Is Infected

Since this book is intended for the typical computer user, and not the highly experienced computer technician, this chapter will present only the most straightforward, safest steps to take in an effort to remove a virus infection and repair any damage that the malware may have caused.

In cases of a simple virus infection that has been widely distributed and well documented, there is a good chance that you can eliminate the virus yourself, without the need for professional help. But if the steps outlined in this chapter don't solve the problem, your most prudent course of action would be to turn the infected computer over to someone experienced in the inner workings of virus eradication.

## Turn Off the Computer

If you intend to have someone else work on the infestation, the first step you can take to limit the damage is to turn the computer off until it is safely in the hands of a competent virus-repair technician. As long as the computer is powered on, the virus can keep spreading and cause even more damage while you wait for a diagnosis.

If you feel that you must keep using the computer, in spite of the apparent virus infection, it should at least be disconnected from the Internet. This precaution will prevent any further infection, and will keep the computer in question from infecting others via e-mail.

## Disconnect From the Network

As a further step in isolating the infected computer, if it is connected to other computers on a Local-Area Network, or LAN, disconnect that cable as well. Most modern viruses will attempt to spread to other computers on the LAN, so this step will prevent the spread of the virus within your home or office environment.

## Delete Temporary Internet Files

In many cases, a virus-infected or worm-bearing file is stored on your hard drive in the Temporary Internet Files area. It's good housekeeping to clear these files periodically, and there's no better time than when you're dealing with a virus infection.

The safest way to delete these files is through the provisions included in your Web browser program. In the case of Internet Explorer, you access this feature by clicking on Internet Options... under the Tools menu.

In the dialog box that comes up there, look on the General tab for the section titled "Temporary Internet files," and click on Delete Files... In that box, check the option that says "Delete all offline content," and then click OK. You may see the hourglass for a few minutes while these files are being deleted, but be patient. There could easily be tens of thousands of these files, and it can take a while to delete all of them.

After taking this step, try running your AV scan again, and see whether there are still virus-infected files on the computer. If not, you can be satisfied that those files were in the Temporary Internet Files area, and you have successfully deleted them.

If the infected files are still present, it is possible that they could not be deleted because they were in use at the time. To reduce this possibility, restart Windows in Safe Mode and delete the Temporary Internet Files again. Then run the AV scan one more time, and see whether you've eliminated the offending programs this way.

## Try System Restore (Windows XP Only)

The System Restore feature of Windows XP provides the ability to "turn back the clock" to a previous date and time and thus undo changes that did not produce the desired result. In some cases it is possible to use this feature to restore the computer to its condition prior to the virus infection.

On the other hand, it may be necessary to disable the System Restore function in order to fully remove a virus from an infected system. When in doubt, leave this capability intact for the best chance of fairly straightforward recovery from virus damage.

If you have chosen to use a third-party utility program such as Goback, there is a very good chance that you can recover from any virus infection by restoring the system to a date prior to the time it became infected.

## Check For a Removal Tool

If you have been able to determine, by name, the exact virus that has infected your computer, there is a good chance that a removal tool is available for that specific virus. If you have this information, go to the Technical Support area of your AV software vendor's Web site and do a search for the designated virus name.

In most cases, this search will return instructions for removal of the specified virus and, in some cases, steps for repairing the damage caused by the virus. For the more widespread viruses, there may be a removal tool that you can download to repair the damage automatically, and completely remove the virus from your computer.

While the instructions provided for removal of specific viruses are a good starting point, it is not uncommon for them to be incomplete. In the rush to post removal instructions on the Web site, the AV vendors sometimes don't have all of the relevant information at hand when they develop the procedure.

## Keep Checking

If you've applied the prescribed procedure and see an improvement, but there still seem to be pieces of the virus lingering on the system, you would be well advised to check the vendor's Web site again the next day for a more recent procedure. Especially when a virus is spreading rapidly, the AV software vendors frequently update their removal procedure as they learn more about that particular virus.

## Delete the Infected Message from the Mail Server

If you're accessing your e-mail through a dial-up connection and receive an e-mail message with a virus, it may appear to keep coming back. If this happens to you, it may be necessary to delete the infected message from the Mail Server in order to get past that message to the next one in line.

Depending upon your Internet Service Provider, or your Mail Host, you may have the ability to delete messages from the Mail Server yourself, or you may have to request that the message be deleted for you by someone responsible for the Mail Server.

## Add Filters to Your E-Mail Program

In some cases of repetitive e-mail messages containing viruses, you may find it practical to use the filters in your e-mail program to prevent these messages from being downloaded to your computer. If you are using Microsoft Outlook as your e-mail program (as opposed to Outlook Express), you have the ability to filter out messages before they are downloaded.

Depending on the nature of the particular virus, it may always have a specific Subject that you can put into a filter, or it may always appear to come from a specific e-mail address that can be filtered out. Filters such as these can greatly reduce the amount of time you need to spend removing viruses that would have come through otherwise.

Filters, also known as Mail Rules, are covered in detail in Chapter 9, "Dealing With Spam." The examples included are from Microsoft's Outlook and Outlook Express e-mail programs, but most e-mail programs will offer comparable capabilities.

## What About Help From Microsoft?

A Frequently Asked Question about dealing with virus infection is, "Why not get Microsoft to fix it?" While this would be a simple solution if it worked, that is rarely the case. Microsoft generally takes the position that virus infection isn't their problem, that the user should have taken the steps necessary to protect their computer from a virus infection in the first place.

Even so, there is some useful information about virus prevention on the Microsoft KnowledgeBase. Especially when you know the name of the virus that is causing your problems, a search of the KnowledgeBase will frequently provide useful information on that particular virus.

## Reformat Your Hard Drive?

One piece of advice that is offered all too often, in the face of a virus infection, is to reformat the hard drive and start all over. While that approach could solve the problems directly related to malware, it could also introduce a whole new range of problems related to programs that had been installed and data files created since the computer was new.

## A Better Alternative – Your Restore CD

An alternative that could be worth considering is to use the Restore CD that came with the computer. This disk may offer the option of repairing specific damage, or just reinstalling the Windows Operating System, but more typically it wipes out everything on the hard drive and restores the computer to the way it looked when it first was removed from the box.

If you do choose to restore the computer to its original configuration, be sure to back up all of your data files first, and find the original installation disks or CDs for all the software that will need to be reinstalled.

Remember that if you go this route, you will also need to reapply all Windows Updates, reinstall and update your AV and/or Firewall software, provide the current drivers for any hardware devices that have been added to the system, and reset your preferences and default settings.

Of course, your Internet Connection and e-mail settings will need to be set up again as well. This includes your Favorites and Address Book, so be sure and back up those files before loading the Restore CD.

## When Virus Removal Isn't That Simple

If the problem you're facing doesn't respond to the steps in this chapter, it will probably be necessary for you to take the compromised computer to a trained professional. The virus-removal techniques that probably will be required at this stage could cause permanent damage to your computer if applied improperly.

At any rate, if you've made your way through these procedures to this point, you can have the satisfaction of knowing you've done everything reasonably possible to repair the damage on your own.

On the other hand, if you have solved the problem without outside assistance, you have every right to be very proud of yourself. Removing viruses and other forms of malware, and repairing the damage they cause, is one of the most difficult challenges faced by computer professionals. Congratulations!

# Appendix
## Country Codes, Listed Alphabetically

| | | | | |
|---|---|---|---|---|
| AD | Andorra | | BO | Bolivia |
| AE | United Arab Emirates | | BR | Brazil |
| AF | Afghanistan | | BS | Bahamas |
| AG | Antigua and Barbuda | | BT | Bhutan |
| AI | Anguilla | | BV | Bouvet Island |
| AL | Albania | | BW | Botswana |
| AM | Armenia | | BY | Belarus |
| AN | Netherlands Antilles | | BZ | Belize |
| AO | Angola | | CA | Canada |
| AQ | Antarctica | | CC | Cocos (Keeling) Islands |
| AR | Argentina | | CF | Central African Republic |
| AS | American Samoa | | CG | Congo |
| AT | Austria | | CH | Switzerland |
| AU | Australia | | CI | Cote D'Ivoire (Ivory Coast) |
| AW | Aruba | | CK | Cook Islands |
| AZ | Azerbaijan | | CL | Chile |
| BA | Bosnia and Herzegovina | | CM | Cameroon |
| BB | Barbados | | CN | China |
| BD | Bangladesh | | CO | Colombia |
| BE | Belgium | | CR | Costa Rica |
| BF | Burkina Faso | | CS | Czechoslovakia (former) |
| BG | Bulgaria | | CU | Cuba |
| BH | Bahrain | | CV | Cape Verde |
| BI | Burundi | | CX | Christmas Island |
| BJ | Benin | | CY | Cyprus |
| BM | Bermuda | | CZ | Czech Republic |
| BN | Brunei Darussalam | | DE | Germany |

| | | | |
|---|---|---|---|
| EG | Egypt | HU | Hungary |
| EH | Western Sahara | ID | Indonesia |
| ER | Eritrea | IE | Ireland |
| ES | Spain | IL | Israel |
| ET | Ethiopia | IN | India |
| FI | Finland | IO | British Indian Ocean Territory |
| FJ | Fiji | IQ | Iraq |
| FK | Falkland Islands (Malvinas) | IR | Iran |
| FM | Micronesia | IS | Iceland |
| FO | Faroe Islands | IT | Italy |
| FR | France | JM | Jamaica |
| FX | France, Metropolitan | JO | Jordan |
| GA | Gabon | JP | Japan |
| GB | Great Britain (UK) | KE | Kenya |
| GD | Grenada | KG | Kyrgyzstan |
| GE | Georgia | KH | Cambodia |
| GF | French Guiana | KI | Kiribati |
| GH | Ghana | KM | Comoros |
| GI | Gibraltar | KN | Saint Kitts and Nevis |
| GL | Greenland | KP | Korea (North) |
| GM | Gambia | KR | Korea (South) |
| GN | Guinea | KW | Kuwait |
| GP | Guadeloupe | KY | Cayman Islands |
| GQ | Equatorial Guinea | KZ | Kazakhstan |
| GR | Greece | LA | Laos |
| GS | S. Georgia and S. Sandwich Isls. | LB | Lebanon |
| GT | Guatemala | LC | Saint Lucia |
| GU | Guam | LI | Liechtenstein |
| GW | Guinea-Bissau | LK | Sri Lanka |
| GY | Guyana | LR | Liberia |
| HK | Hong Kong | LS | Lesotho |
| HM | Heard and McDonald Islands | LT | Lithuania |
| HN | Honduras | LU | Luxembourg |
| HR | Croatia (Hrvatska) | LV | Latvia |
| HT | Haiti | LY | Libya |

| | | | |
|---|---|---|---|
| MA | Morocco | PA | Panama |
| MC | Monaco | PE | Peru |
| MD | Moldova | PF | French Polynesia |
| MG | Madagascar | PG | Papua New Guinea |
| MH | Marshall Islands | PH | Philippines |
| MK | Macedonia | PK | Pakistan |
| ML | Mali | PL | Poland |
| MM | Myanmar | PM | St. Pierre and Miquelon |
| MN | Mongolia | PN | Pitcairn |
| MO | Macau | PR | Puerto Rico |
| MP | Northern Mariana Islands | PT | Portugal |
| MQ | Martinique | PW | Palau |
| MR | Mauritania | PY | Paraguay |
| MS | Montserrat | QA | Qatar |
| MT | Malta | RE | Reunion |
| MU | Mauritius | RO | Romania |
| MV | Maldives | RU | Russian Federation |
| MW | Malawi | RW | Rwanda |
| MX | Mexico | SA | Saudi Arabia |
| MY | Malaysia | SB | Solomon Islands |
| MZ | Mozambique | SC | Seychelles |
| NA | Namibia | SD | Sudan |
| NC | New Caledonia | SE | Sweden |
| NE | Niger | SG | Singapore |
| NF | Norfolk Island | SH | St. Helena |
| NG | Nigeria | SI | Slovenia |
| NI | Nicaragua | SJ | Svalbard and Jan Mayen Islands |
| NL | Netherlands | SK | Slovak Republic |
| NO | Norway | SL | Sierra Leone |
| NP | Nepal | SM | San Marino |
| NR | Nauru | SN | Senegal |
| NT | Neutral Zone | SO | Somalia |
| NU | Niue | SR | Suriname |
| NZ | New Zealand (Aotearoa) | ST | Sao Tome and Principe |
| OM | Oman | SU | USSR (former) |

| | | | |
|---|---|---|---|
| SV | El Salvador | YE | Yemen |
| SY | Syria | YT | Mayotte |
| SZ | Swaziland | YU | Yugoslavia |
| TC | Turks and Caicos Islands | ZA | South Africa |
| TD | Chad | ZM | Zambia |
| TF | French Southern Territories | ZR | Zaire |
| TG | Togo | ZW | Zimbabwe |
| TH | Thailand | COM | US Commercial |
| TJ | Tajikistan | EDU | US Educational |
| TK | Tokelau | GOV | US Government |
| TM | Turkmenistan | INT | International |
| TN | Tunisia | MIL | US Military |
| TO | Tonga | NET | Network |
| TP | East Timor | ORG | Non-Profit Organization |
| TR | Turkey | ARPA | Old style Arpanet |
| TT | Trinidad and Tobago | NATO | NATO field |
| TV | Tuvalu | | |
| TW | Taiwan | | |
| TZ | Tanzania | | |
| UA | Ukraine | | |
| UG | Uganda | | |
| UK | United Kingdom | | |
| UM | US Minor Outlying Islands | | |
| US | United States | | |
| UY | Uruguay | | |
| UZ | Uzbekistan | | |
| VA | Vatican City State (Holy See) | | |
| VC | Saint Vincent and the Grenadines | | |
| VE | Venezuela | | |
| VG | Virgin Islands (British) | | |
| VI | Virgin Islands (U.S.) | | |
| VN | Viet Nam | | |
| VU | Vanuatu | | |
| WF | Wallis and Futuna Islands | | |
| WS | Samoa | | |

# Appendix B
## Unsafe File List, from Microsoft

Microsoft has identified over 40 File Types that could contain viruses or other malicious codes. The complete list can be found in Knowledge-Base Article 291369, at the following address: http://support.microsoft.com/default.aspx?scid=kb;en-us;291369

Here are the file extensions included in the Unsafe File List:

| | | |
|---|---|---|
| .ad | .isp | .shb |
| .adp | .js | .shs |
| .asp | .jse | .url |
| .bas | .lnk | .vb |
| .bat | .mdb | .vbe |
| .chm | .mde | .vbs |
| .cmd | .msc | .vsd |
| .com | .msi | .vss |
| .cpl | .msp | .vst |
| .crt | .mst | .vsw |
| .exe | .pcd | .ws |
| .hlp | .pif | .wsc |
| .hta | .reg | .wsf |
| .inf | .scr | .wsh |
| .ins | .sct | |

# Appendix C
## Keeping This Information Current

The world has never experienced an industry that changes as dramatically and as frequently as computers. And within this environment of rapid change, the producers of viruses and other forms of malware are the leaders of the pack.

Trying to stay ahead of the potential problems posed by these cyber-terrorists may be too much to ask. But if you can stay reasonably current with the latest forms of attack, the most recent virus definitions, and the newest replication techniques, you stand the best chance of preventing a successful attack on your computer.

By registering your copy of this book, you may download monthly updates and keep the information current. Each update will highlight the most significant new viruses, the most appropriate defense against these threats, and any new vulnerabilities that have been identified.

You are entitled to twelve monthly updates at no additional charge. After a year, you can decide whether to renew your update service, for a nominal fee.

Registration also allows you to download a document that contains "live" hyperlinks to the various Web sites referenced in this book. This bonus document can save you lots of keystrokes when you want more detailed information on the topics presented here, or when you want to go directly to a vendor's Web site for any reason.

In addition, you'll find some surprises in the Registration area that can help you along your path to Bug-Free Computing.

To receive all these benefits and bonus materials, log on to http://www.thevirusdoc.com and go to the Registration page. Enter the requested information, and use the following code for your Product ID:

### BFC1008001

Thank you for your purchase, and may all your Computing be Bug-Free!